Reshaping
Government
in
Metropolitan
Areas

A Statement

on National Policy

by the Research and Policy Committee

of the Committee for Economic Development

February 1970

CED

37349

Single Copy . . . $1.00

Printed in U.S.A.
First Printing February 1970
Committee for Economic Development
477 Madison Avenue, New York, N.Y.10022
Design: Harry Carter
Cover photograph: Ewing Galloway

Library of Congress Catalog Card Number: 74-114417

Contents

THE RESPONSIBILITY FOR CED

STATEMENTS ON NATIONAL POLICY

This statement has been approved for publication as a statement of the Research and Policy Committee by the members of that Committee and its drafting subcommittee, subject to individual dissents or reservations noted herein. The trustees who are responsible for this statement are listed on the opposite page. Company associations are included for identification only; the companies do not share in the responsibility borne by the individuals.

The Research and Policy Committee is directed by CED's bylaws to:

"Initiate studies into the principles of business policy and of public policy which will foster the full contribution by industry and commerce to the attainment and maintenance of high and secure standards of living for people in all walks of life through maximum employment and high productivity in the domestic economy."

The bylaws emphasize that:

"All research is to be thoroughly objective in character, and the approach in each instance is to be from the standpoint of the general welfare and not from that of any special political or economic group."

The Research and Policy Committee is composed of 50 Trustees from among the 200 businessmen and educators who comprise the Committee for Economic Development. It is aided by a Research Advisory Board of leading economists, a small permanent Research Staff, and by advisors chosen for their competence in the field being considered.

Each Statement on National Policy is preceded by discussions, meetings, and exchanges of memoranda, often stretching over many months. The research is undertaken by a subcommittee, with its advisors, and the full Research and Policy Committee participates in the drafting of findings and recommendations.

Except for the members of the Research and Policy Committee and the responsible subcommittee, the recommendations presented herein are not necessarily endorsed by other Trustees or by the advisors, contributors, staff members, or others associated with CED.

The Research and Policy Committee offers these Statements on National Policy as an aid to clearer understanding of the steps to be taken in achieving sustained growth of the American economy. The Committee is not attempting to pass on any pending specific legislative proposals; its purpose is to urge careful consideration of the objectives set forth in the statement and of the best means of accomplishing those objectives.

4.

5.

6.

Foreword

CED's Research and Policy Committee has long been concerned with the ways in which organization and structure affect the ability of governments to manage the public's business. In recent years, the Committee has issued a number of statements that propose policies for improving government at all levels in our federal system. For example, *Modernizing Local Government* (1966) calls for substantial consolidation of the nation's fragmented municipal governments. *A Fiscal Program for a Balanced Federalism* (1967) recommends methods of strengthening federal-state-local fiscal relations. *Modernizing State Government* (1967) urges a major overhaul of state governments and their constitutions.

The present statement, *Reshaping Government in Metropolitan Areas,* is timely and significant on several counts. First, it examines the impact of governmental structure on the lives of citizens and demonstrates that the existing organization of metropolitan government

7.

can be a serious impediment to the solution of problems of the central city and the suburbs. Second, it responds forthrightly to the growing and often conflicting demands for a governmental system capable of dealing with metropolitan-wide problems on the one hand and community problems on the other. It recognizes, along the lines of *Modernizing Local Government,* that increasingly there are problems that spill beyond the boundaries of local communities and that these problems can only be dealt with by a larger, metropolitan-wide jurisdiction. But within this context it makes plain the need for a smaller unit of government which would allow citizens of local communities to control and manage their own affairs. Finally, it emphasizes the importance of federal and state encouragement and support. The federal government and the states are called upon to develop programs that are relevant to the needs of metropolitan areas and to adjust their financial assistance accordingly.

This statement is not meant to cover the many substantive problems of metropolitan areas, but to provide a modern framework for solutions to problems of welfare, jobs for the hard-core unemployed, and education for the disadvantaged—all of these subjects now on this Committee's agenda.

Reshaping Government in Metropolitan Areas was prepared by a subcommittee under the chairmanship of Philip M. Klutznick. Dr. Alan K. Campbell, Dean of The Maxwell Graduate School of Citizenship and Public Affairs, Syracuse University, was Project Director. The members of the subcommittee and its advisors are listed on pages 5 and 6. On behalf of the Research and Policy Committee, I want to express thanks to Mr. Klutznick, Dr. Campbell, and the subcommittee for their valuable contributions. We are also indebted to William H. Wilken for providing research assistance; C. Peter Clute for preparing the Appendices on "Metropolitanism" and "The Metropolitan Toronto Experience"; and Sol Hurwitz, CED's Director of Information, for providing editorial assistance.

Emilio G. Collado, *Chairman*
Research and Policy Committee

1. Introduction and Summary of Recommendations

Metropolitan areas embrace most of our greatest resources. They are centers of commerce and industry, fashion, culture, and thought. Many metropolitan areas are wealthier and more populous than most nations.

Yet metropolitan America is in trouble. In cities and suburbs alike, citizens are beset by complexities that disturb their everyday lives. They are threatened by crime in the streets, by impure air and water, by breakdowns in public transportation. They are burdened by high taxes and inflationary prices. The deprived minorities in the slums and ghettos suffer more than other citizens of metropolis, for they are more likely to be jobless or sick, badly educated or poorly housed. What is worse, they are handicapped by racial discrimination in their efforts to improve their own condition.

Vigorous leadership is essential if the plight of metropolitan Americans of all races—in cities and suburbs—is to improve. The national and state governments must develop relevant substantive programs designed to deal with a host of diverse and elusive metropolitan problems. At the same time, metropolitan areas must develop a system of government that is capable—administratively, fiscally, and politically —of translating substantive programs into action. Such a system must be

9.

geared to respond not only to problems of metropolitan-wide concern, but to those of local communities within metropolitan areas.

We do not intend in this statement to recommend substantive policies and programs to meet the many problems of metropolitan America. Proposals for dealing with some of these difficulties may be found in earlier CED statements; proposals for dealing with others will appear in statements now under way by the Research and Policy Committee. Our purpose here is to provide guidelines for redesigning the present structure and organization of government in metropolitan areas. Without a more rational, more flexible system than now exists—one that recognizes local as well as area-wide needs—new policies and programs are likely to fail.*

The structure of government in metropolitan areas has a profound impact on the daily lives of metropolitan citizens. But, as this Committee has long recognized, the present arrangement of overlapping local units is not serving the people well.[1] Citizens in metropolitan areas are confronted by a confusing maze of many—possibly a dozen—jurisdictions, each with its own bureaucratic labyrinth. This baffling array of local units has made it difficult for citizens—the disadvantaged particularly—to gain access to public services and to acquire a voice in decision-making.

Clearly, a fragmented system of government works better for some than for others. In gaining access to the system, citizens with greater political influence and sophistication may succeed in bypassing bureaucratic governmental procedures. Moreover, the system generally works better for suburbanites than it does for residents of the central cities. The haphazard arrangement of local governments in metropolitan areas has created great inequalities between resources and needs. In the suburbs, the combination of superior fiscal strength and fewer problems usually yields a higher quality of public service; in the central cities the situation is reversed. But it is not entirely by chance that such disparities have developed. One of the principal failings of a fragmented system of government is its inability to take an overview in matters of planning, transportation, and population dispersal. Zoning and other land-use control powers wielded by small suburban communities tend to exclude from the suburbs black citizens and other low-income minority groups.

1/See *Modernizing Local Government*, a Statement on National Policy by the Research and Policy Committee, Committee for Economic Development, New York, July 1966.

*See Memorandum by MR. ALLAN SPROUL, *page 57*.

10.

Fragmented local governments reflect great variations in character and viewpoint. The fact that fragmentation persists indicates a determination among local communities to control their own affairs and preserve their own identities. While this attitude makes for greater local pride, it also results in failure of local communities to unite on matters of area-wide concern, such as environmental pollution and transportation congestion, which seriously undermine the quality of metropolitan life. The question to which this statement is addressed may be stated quite simply:

Can existing forms of government in metropolitan areas be modified to permit solution of area-wide problems and at the same time permit local communities to manage their own affairs and maintain their own identities?

Metropolitan Trends[1]

Mounting population pressures which accelerated after World War II have sent Americans beyond their central cities in a quest for space. At the same time, there have been pressures in the opposite direction: the technological revolution in agriculture has forced residents of rural areas to abandon the farms and move in great numbers to the cities. This dual movement has intensified the problems of metropolitan areas.

The cities have suffered the most. The departure of business firms and a large proportion of the more affluent, white residents to the suburbs has severely weakened the cities' tax base. This, in turn, has made it more difficult for cities to deal with problems of race and poverty brought on by a heavy influx of poor, nonwhite residents. But the suburbs have suffered, too. The worsening condition of the cities has only speeded the outward movement, and the result has been many problems of the cities have spread beyond their borders. Suburbanites found that governmental patterns designed for rural areas were not suited to their needs. To cope with new problems, new governments were created, but they were not created with a rational view to the future. Rather, they seemed to spring up—in endless proliferation. These new governments, tacked on to one another around the central city, have formed the crazy-quilt that is metropolitan America today.

1/For details, see Appendix A, p. 63.

The U.S. Bureau of the Budget defines a metropolitan area as "an integrated economic and social unit with a recognized large population nucleus." These units are called "standard metropolitan statistical areas" (SMSA's), defined by the Budget Bureau as normally consisting of one or more entire counties, primarily nonagricultural and closely related to and including a central city, or cities, of 50,000 or more. Nearly two-thirds of the U.S. population is concentrated today in 233 metropolitan areas compared with only 55 per cent in 1940. Until the mid-1960's a majority of the residents of metropolitan areas lived in central cities; now the preponderance has shifted to the suburbs. (See Figure One.)

Growth is still generally toward metropolitan areas. Between 1960

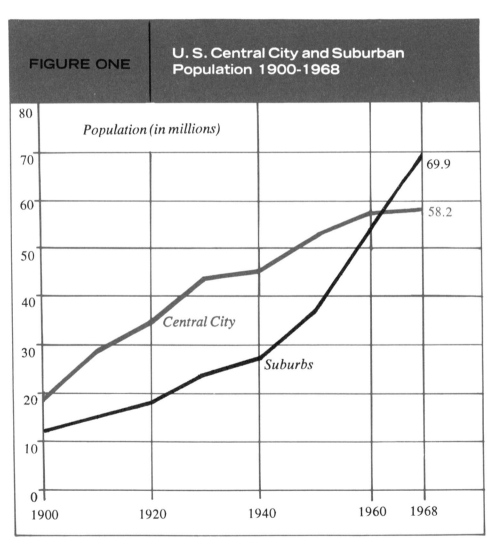

FIGURE ONE | **U. S. Central City and Suburban Population 1900-1968**

Source: U.S. Bureau of the Census.

12.

and 1966 their population increased 11 per cent compared to 6 per cent for nonmetropolitan areas. By 1985 it is projected that more than 70 per cent of the population will live in metropolitan areas. The metropolitan areas of the Northeast represent the largest concentration of metropolitan population in the United States: they account for 79 per cent of the region's total population. The metropolitan areas of the West account for 72 per cent of the region's total population and are the fastest growing. Metropolitan population concentration in the North Central region is 60 per cent; in the South, 48 per cent.

There are metropolitan areas in 47 of the 50 states. Alaska, Vermont, and Wyoming have no population now defined as metropolitan. Eight states have at least 80 per cent of their population in metropolitan areas. These are led by Massachusetts with 97 per cent and California with 90 per cent. However, 28 states have less than 50 per cent of their population in metropolitan areas. (See Figure Two and Figure Three.)

At last count, there were 455 metropolitan counties. Nearly half of the nation's metropolitan areas consist of a single county. Fifteen metropolitan areas consist of five counties or more.

In 1967 the nation's metropolitan areas were served by 20,703 local governments, or about one-fourth of all the local governments in the United States. The average is 91 local governments per metropolitan area—46 per metropolitan county. But these averages cover great extremes. The Chicago metropolitan area, for example, has 1,113 local governments (186 per county); the Philadelphia area has 871 (109 per county); the Pittsburgh area has 704 (176 per county); and the New York area has 551 (110 per county). At the other extreme there are 20 metropolitan areas with less than 10 local governments each.

In both population and physical size most local governments in metropolitan areas are extremely small. For example, two-thirds of the municipalities (usually cities, boroughs, villages, or towns) have a population of less than 5,000, and about half cover less than a single square mile of land area. Fewer than 200 municipalities cover as much as 25 square miles.

Most metropolitan residents are served by at least four separate local governments—a county, a municipality or a township, a school district, and one or more special districts whose functions range from garbage collection to mosquito control. Some, of course, are served by many more. The residents of Blue Island, Illinois, must contend with 13 separate, independent local governments.

13.

FIGURE TWO: Standard Metropolitan Statistical Areas Defined by U.S. Bureau of the Budget to May 1, 1969

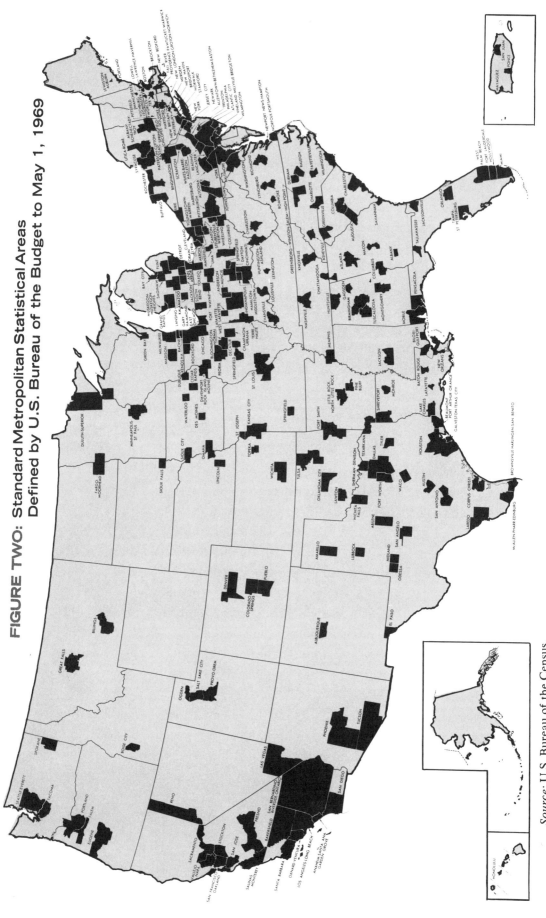

Source: U.S. Bureau of the Census.

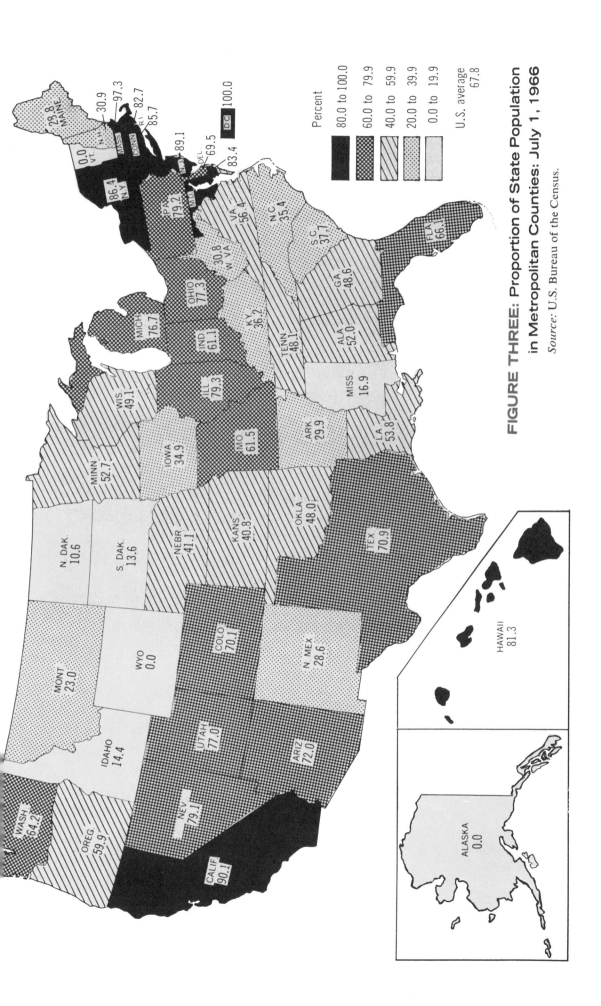

FIGURE THREE: Proportion of State Population
in Metropolitan Counties: July 1, 1966

Source: U.S. Bureau of the Census.

Percent

80.0 to 100.0

60.0 to 79.9

40.0 to 59.9

20.0 to 39.9

0.0 to 19.9

U.S. average
67.8

MAINE 28.8
N.H. 30.9
VT. 0.0
MASS. 97.3
CONN. 82.7
R.I. 85.7
N.Y. 86.4
PA. 79.2
N.J. 89.1
DEL. 69.5
MD. 83.4
D.C. 100.0
VA. 56.4
W.VA. 30.8
N.C. 35.4
S.C. 37.1
GA. 48.6
FLA. 66.1
OHIO 77.3
MICH. 76.7
IND. 61.1
KY. 36.2
TENN. 48.1
ALA. 52.0
MISS. 16.9
WIS. 49.1
ILL. 79.3
MO. 61.5
ARK. 29.9
LA. 53.8
MINN. 52.7
IOWA 34.9
NEBR. 41.1
KANS. 40.8
OKLA. 48.0
TEX. 70.9
N. DAK. 10.6
S. DAK. 13.6
MONT. 23.0
WYO. 0.0
COLO. 70.1
N MEX. 28.6
IDAHO 14.4
UTAH 77.0
ARIZ. 72.0
WASH. 64.2
OREG. 59.9
NEV. 79.1
CALIF. 90.1
HAWAII 81.3
ALASKA 0.0

Steps Toward Reform

In *Modernizing Local Government*, this Committee underscored the need for local government reform as follows:

The bewildering multiplicity of small, piecemeal, duplicative, overlapping local jurisdictions cannot cope with the staggering difficulties encountered in managing modern urban affairs. The fiscal effects of duplicative suburban separatism create great difficulty in provision of costly central city services benefiting the whole urbanized area. If local governments are to function effectively in metropolitan areas, they must have sufficient size and authority to plan, administer, and provide significant financial support for solutions to area-wide problems.[1]

To this end we recommended reducing through consolidation the number of conflicting jurisdictions and competing tax units. We also proposed that county governments—because they are less limited in area, population, and fiscal resources—be utilized where possible as the primary basis for consolidation.

Aware of the need for change, enlightened business and civic leaders in metropolitan areas have spearheaded campaigns to replace small-scale, overlapping local governments with consolidated, federated, or other forms of metropolitan government. These campaigns have stressed the fact that the economic and social interdependence of metropolitan areas has created problems which can only be solved on an area-wide basis.

Centralization vs. Decentralization

Steps in the direction of area-wide government are not surprising when considered in their historical context. For nearly two centuries, American government has become increasingly centralized. Cities have expanded their boundaries by annexation. States have assumed new functions or have taken more responsibility for old ones. The national government has broadened its role in domestic affairs. Traditionally, much support for centralization has been based on the assumption that it leads to better, more responsive government and more humane social policies.

1/*Modernizing Local Government, op. cit.,* p. 44.

It may seem paradoxical, therefore, that today's growing support for decentralization should rest upon the same assumption. Much of the popular discussion of decentralization centers on current demands of black citizens for control over those institutions which most affect their lives, and for a stronger voice in the political process. The dialogue over black community control has focused public attention on many legitimate grievances of black citizens. The issue of decentralization, however, is not limited to the black community. White citizens, too, are impelled toward decentralized government (witness the suburban village) by some of the same factors that are motivating blacks: a desire for greater separatism and a stronger sense of local pride and community identity. Indeed, decentralization goes beyond questions of black and white. Its advocates see it as a means of humanizing government, giving the voter greater access to public services, more control over the bureaucracy which manages his affairs, and a more important role in decisions in which he has a stake.

The case for decentralization, however, cannot ignore the economic, technological, and social arguments which favor a centralized system. Small-unit governments are poorly equipped to take advantage of economies of scale and technological innovations; hence, they often find it more difficult to respond to the growing and disparate needs of their citizens. Proponents of centralization argue that the interests of the disadvantaged are best served by a larger rather than a smaller unit of government. They point to the economic weakness of the ghetto, the historic conservatism of America's small communities, and the growing dependence on the federal government for social progress.

It is clear from the foregoing that what is needed is a system of government that adequately recognizes *both* forces, centralization and decentralization. Such a system must permit a genuine sharing of power over functions between a larger unit and a smaller unit. It must recognize a larger unit to permit economies of scale, area-wide planning, and equities in finance. It must recognize a smaller unit to permit the exercise of local power over matters which affect the lives of local citizens.

Some basic arrangements for sharing responsibility and power for individual functions between area-wide governments and community districts are outlined in Chapter 4. For each there is an area-wide component and a local component. However, no hard lines have been drawn between functions or even parts of functions or between levels of government. The emphasis is on the *sharing of power* and not on the assignment of entire functions to either level.

SUMMARY OF RECOMMENDATIONS*

All metropolitan areas are affected to a greater or lesser extent by the conflicting forces of centralization and decentralization. The interdependence of activities within metropolitan areas requires area-wide institutions for some functions or parts of functions of government. Just as clear is the need for units of government small enough to enable the recipients of government services to have some voice and control over their quality and quantity.

However, no two metropolitan areas are alike. Each has its own history and life style, and its own economic base. Both demographically and geographically, each differs from the other. For this reason, our proposals will not apply alike to all metropolitan areas. Each must examine its own capacity to govern and determine what particular organization suits it best.

It has been argued that the present governmental system already possesses the necessary combination of smallness and bigness. Small government already exists, at least in suburbia, and when area-wide action is needed, special districts may be created for the purpose. Further, the present system could govern effectively, it is often claimed, if only it had enough money.

None of these justifications for the present system is satisfactory. Uncoordinated area-wide special districts, fragmented by function, are no better than governments fragmented geographically. They do not permit a genuine regional approach to problems that are genuinely regional; nor do they create a system of decision-making and power-sharing capable of dealing with political conflicts. The state and federal aid solution within the present system has already been tried and so far has been found wanting.[1] Aid is badly allocated. Often it is wasted or assigned without proper priorities.

1/See *A Fiscal Program for a Balanced Federalism*, a Statement on National Policy by the Research and Policy Committee, Committee for Economic Development, New York, June 1967.
*See Memorandum by MR. PHILIP SPORN, *page 58.*

A Two-Level Governmental System

In principle a governmental system for America's metropolitan areas must recognize the need for both a community level and a metropolitan level of government. There are many different governmental arrangements which will meet this need. As long as legitimate demands for centralization and decentralization are met, the specific arrangements may vary to fit the economic, cultural, and political characteristics of each area. Some may require greater emphasis on consolidation of local units; others may require greater emphasis on creating units which will enhance community participation.

Therefore, in the following proposals to achieve the dual advantages of a combined community-metropolitan governmental system, we would expect variations in application. In some areas a comprehensive solution may be feasible at an early date. In other areas achievement of an effective two-level system may require several steps over a period of time.

To gain the advantages of both centralization and decentralization, we recommend as an ultimate solution a governmental system of two levels. Some functions should be assigned in their entirety to the area-wide government, others to the local level, but most will be assigned in part to each level.* More important than the division of functions is the *sharing of power*. Local communities will be assigned some power over functions placed at the area-wide level of government. Further, state and federal governments must be involved in most functions. This two-level system will not provide neatness and symmetry, but effectiveness, responsiveness, and adequate resources.

In those situations where the metropolitan area is contained within one county, a reconstituted county government should be used as the basic framework for a new area-wide government. This may, but need not, include consolidation of a large dominant central city with the county government in which it is located. If there are two or more sizable cities in the county, consolidation may not be appropriate. Counties in some states already have very wide powers. An indispensable requirement is the restructuring of such counties with a suitable legislative organ, a strong chief executive, and modern management.

In cases where the metropolitan area spreads over several counties

---

*See Memorandum by MR. HERMAN L. WEISS, *page 59.*

or towns, a new jurisdiction should be created which embraces all of its territory. Although a federation of existing counties and towns might be considerably easier to implement, it is clear that rapid metropolitan growth makes a stronger jurisdiction considerably more appropriate, especially for purposes of long-range planning.

In addition to an area-wide level, modern metropolitan government should contain a community-level government system comprised of "community districts." These units might consist of existing local governments with functions readjusted to the two-level system, together with new districts in areas where no local unit exists. The new community districts should not be imposed from without, but created through local initiative by the simplest possible methods. A state boundary commission or similar body might be established to begin the process of delineating new districts. Citizen groups which seek community-district status might first make their appeal to this body if it is established.

In some cities there are areas which already possess strong community identity and these could become the new community districts. But in many cities, particularly the big cities, the sense of community is diminishing. Isolation and alienation, on the other hand, are increasing. Once the smaller political units are created—units with genuine power— a stronger sense of community is bound to emerge. In the suburbs, existing municipalities are likely to be retained as the community districts. Except in the most recently settled suburbs, these municipalities tend not only to represent "natural areas," but also to have well-developed community identities. Thus, local communities in both cities and suburbs can be guaranteed full participation within the metropolitan system.

Determining Size

A major difficulty in establishing community districts will be determining their size. Although much of the literature on government organization places heavy emphasis on appropriate size of minor jurisdictions, the fact is there is little hard economic evidence of what the optimum size should be. Therefore, how a community perceives its identity becomes important as well as the number of people it contains.

States should establish suggested, but not mandatory, criteria to guide the actual determination of community boundaries. The states should, in addition, set down requirements which will guarantee the rep-

20.

resentativeness of the government established. **Although the community districts should be allowed to determine their form of government—council, strong executive, commission, or some other form—the basic requirement of one-man, one-vote should be met.***

State governments should assist the organization of community districts by enacting enabling legislation to permit the creation of a two-level form of metropolitan government and by establishing a procedure through which community districts may be created. Great flexibility as to size and governmental organization should be permitted.

The states should also prescribe guidelines for determining size and representation of the area-wide government. The practice exists in some metropolitan areas of representing community units—towns and villages—on an area-wide governing council. However, this form of representation rarely produces an area-wide point of view but rather a bargaining process through which the various smaller units try to protect their parochial interests. Therefore, we suggest that delegates to the area-wide government represent legislative districts on a one-man, one-vote basis instead of representing the community districts as such.

It is important to underline the full significance of the changes advocated here. **City boundaries would become less important than they now are. There would be a boundary surrounding each metropolitan area as well as boundaries surrounding community districts within each metropolitan area.**

Financing the System:
State and Federal Help

Reorganization of government in metropolitan areas will make it possible to increase over-all fiscal resources. America's wealth is concentrated largely in its metropolitan areas and metropolitan-wide government is advocated, in part, so this resource base may be preserved and improved. The existing system of overlapping local governments results in a poor match between needs and resources and perpetuates waste, inefficiency, and confusion.

Although the establishment of metropolitan-wide government will make possible a greater local fiscal contribution, it will by no means

---

*See Memorandum by MR. ROBERT R. NATHAN, *page 59.*

eliminate the need for substantial state and federal aid. **There is urgent need for a greater and more equitable state aid contribution and more attention by the states to the adequacy of their local governmental systems.** The states have responsibilities for their local governmental systems. They should adapt their aid systems to the facts of metropolitanism and adjust the boundaries of local governments to fit current realities.

The states have the power to assume functions that are now performed locally, but few have assumed them. In some states, highways and welfare have become a major state responsibility, and a few municipal higher educational institutions have been taken over by the states. But there has been no major reshuffling of responsibilities to ease local fiscal burdens.

The response of the federal government to local fiscal problems has been more positive. The federal aid system, for example, through such programs as urban renewal, aid to education, and the anti-poverty program, is adjusting its assistance programs to the problems of the cities. It is possible that by giving more attention to the flow of aid the federal government will be able to help fill the gap left by the state aid system.

Both state and federal aid systems should be restructured in order to put resources where they are most needed. Equally important, state and federal aid should be used to stimulate government reorganization. The use of aid for this purpose has a precedent in its use in promoting school consolidation by the states. **Therefore, we recommend that state and federal aid should be used as an incentive to promote the kind of restructured government outlined in this statement.**

2. Metropolitan Problems

America's metropolitan problems have produced two relatively separate streams of suggestions for reform. One is concerned with substantive problems—education, transportation, housing, welfare, pollution. The other analyzes the structure that governs metropolitan areas. Although the interrelationship between structure and substance is occasionally mentioned, it is seldom analyzed in depth. The result is that the connection between the substantive problems and governmental structure is only vaguely understood.

This policy statement is primarily concerned with the structure and organization of government in metropolitan areas. However, the purpose of the recommended changes is to build a governmental system capable of responding to the substantive problems that plague metropolitan America. The present governmental system often stands in the way of applying new policies, and in some instances, is a significant cause of the problems.

The clearest relationship of governmental structure to the solution of problems can be seen by looking at the impact of the present structure on the availability of resources. As the Introduction indicated, the present fragmented system of government so divides the tax base that frequently resources are most scarce in those jurisdictions which have the most difficult problems. In contrast, there are some areas, particularly in many suburban communities, where resources are plentiful and local problems not numerous.

In addition to the relationship between resources and structure is the equally significant connection between the actual substance of a problem and the governmental system. The dual movement of people and jobs from central city to suburb has produced a distribution of jobs and residences which makes it difficult for many potential manufacturing workers to move from home to job and back. Moreover, in the fields of education, welfare, crime, transportation, and environmental quality, the present governmental system has contributed to the severity of the problems and often stands in the way of the application of at least partial solutions.

Obviously, changes in government structure alone will not solve the substantive problems. There must be relevant policies developed and resources applied. While such policies are outside the scope of this report, it is nevertheless essential for an understanding of the significance of change in governmental structure that we discuss briefly some of the problems that severely limit the quality of metropolitan life. Moreover, the interrelationship of metropolitan problems, resource allocation, and organizational change is reflected in the restructuring recommendations made in the final chapter of this report.

Education

For years the public schools have largely failed to provide pupils in poor metropolitan neighborhoods with the educational preparation required to avoid a life of persistent unemployment or underemployment. Recognizing this, CED in 1965 described improvements in education that would contribute to raising the productivity—and hence the earnings— of many Americans with below average incomes.[1] More recently, in a study on educational research and innovation, the Committee stated:

1/*Raising Low Incomes through Improved Education,* a Statement on National Policy by the Research and Policy Committee, Committee for Economic Development, New York, September 1965.

The schooling of deprived minorities in the slums and ghettos and in many poor rural areas has been a tragic failure and one that will not be corrected without a major revolution in the objectives, methods, and organization of the schools. It will not be corrected until the deprivation of the preschool years is overcome and the child of the slum or ghetto has the capability of gaining basic literacy, nor until the schools are capable of effectively preparing young people for the jobs which industry and business can provide for them.[1]

In another study currently under way, the Committee is addressing itself specifically to improving schooling for the urban disadvantaged.

Since the end of World War II, the quality of schools in poor areas has declined constantly. City schools that were once the best in the nation are now below the quality of most other schools in their own metropolitan areas. A number of reasons for this decline have been suggested by education experts: inadequate resources, the lack of a balanced student population, shortage of modern physical facilities and equipment, and a lack of qualified teachers.

Parents in poverty neighborhoods throughout the country, disgruntled over the inadequacy of their children's education, are pressing for the adoption of wide-ranging school reform measures. Of all the changes demanded, none has met greater opposition than the proposal to divide existing city school systems into many community-controlled districts.

As New York's Ocean Hill-Brownsville dispute revealed, some people resist greater neighborhood control because they believe it is not in their self-interest. Teachers' unions and other groups with a stake in established city school systems, quite understandably, are reluctant to gamble.

Other people, however, stand against increased neighborhood control because they are convinced that it is not in the public interest. Among them are many who fear that the creation of neighborhood-controlled school districts would lead to the reestablishment of *de jure* segregated education. Correctly, they point out that the community school concept is supported not only in poverty neighborhoods, but also

---

1/*Innovation in Education: New Directions for the American School*, a Statement on National Policy by the Research and Policy Committee, Committee for Economic Development, New York, July 1968, p. 12.

in affluent white areas where many residents believe it will eliminate the possibility of racially integrated education. Yet, as proponents of neighborhood schools have observed, integrated education often is not feasible in large cities due to existing and developing residential patterns.

Whether solutions to improved urban education lie in community control or other types of reform, the fact is that unless schools are capable of training young people for life in an urban society, no long-run solution to the urban crisis is possible. The burden which this responsibility places on the schools is heavy, indeed, and it is clear that, in poor areas particularly, they cannot bear it alone. Although the determinants of school performance are not completely understood, it is known that home environment plays an important role. If schools are to function effectively, they will require assistance from those public and private agencies which have responsibility for jobs, housing, welfare, and the general neighborhood environment.

The present fractured government organization in metropolitan areas accentuates the difficulty in providing quality education. It divides resources in a way that makes them least adequate in those school jurisdictions which need them most. Economic and racial integration are discouraged, rather than encouraged, by the present pattern of government.

Welfare

Of all the problems facing central cities today, none is more obviously connected to inadequate educational preparation than rising social dependency. In every state of the nation, socially dependent people are concentrated in the central cities. Consequently, it should not be surprising that New York City has 44.2 per cent of New York State's population, but 70.2 per cent of its public welfare case load. The pattern is the same for America's other large cities.

Fragmented local government is one of the basic institutional causes of the central cities' disproportionate welfare burden. In almost every metropolitan area, suburban communities attempt to minimize their welfare costs by using building codes and zoning ordinances to prevent the construction of private low-cost housing. More importantly, suburban municipalities have beaten back almost every attempt to build publicly-assisted housing within their boundaries. To be sure, much of the central cities' welfare burden stems from institutional causes more powerful than fragmented local government. The most important of these is the welfare system itself. Designed in the late 1930's primarily to eradicate short-term dependency, the welfare system has not been responsive to the needs of an urban society. The result is a system which encourages continuing dependency and places a severe tax burden on those jurisdictions least able to sustain it.

A forthcoming CED policy statement will analyze in detail potential reforms in the public welfare system.

Crime

Like welfare dependency, crime is encouraged by conditions that exist in the central cities' poverty neighborhoods. Nevertheless, today's high crime rates are hardly confined to these places. For example, the National Opinion Research Center estimated that in 1965 crimes against property occurred at a rate of 5,589 per 100,000 population in central cities and at a rate of 5,760 per 100,000 in the suburbs. Similarly, it estimated that crimes against persons occurred at a rate of 2,063 per 100,000 population in the central cities and at a rate of 1,801 in the suburbs.[1]

Despite these similarities between city and suburb, higher over-all crime rates unquestionably exist in the central-city ghettos. Depending on the areas selected for comparison, such rates may be six to ten times higher than in other parts of the cities and in the suburbs.

The growing problem of crime in the central city has heightened public demands for more police patrolling and tougher police action. While blacks and other minority groups view crime in the streets as one of their most important problems, such demands have been met by resentment in certain segments of their communities, particularly among the younger members.

Adequate police protection, whether in suburb or city, is hindered by governmental jurisdictions which tend to block coordinated police action but provide no obstacle to the criminal. Yet neighborhoods and small communities need policemen who understand the community they

---

1/National Opinion Research Center, *Criminal Victimization in the United States*, prepared for the President's Commission on Law Enforcement and Administration of Justice (Washington, D.C.: U.S. Government Printing Office, May 1967).

patrol. This dilemma can be resolved only by a governmental system capable of combining area-wide coverage with local community concern.

Housing

Some grievances cannot be dealt with by local government action alone. One of these is an inadequate supply of standard housing for low- and moderate-income families.

Today many communities, mainly in central cities, are plagued by vermin-ridden, dilapidated housing. In 1960, 8 per cent of central city whites, and 25 per cent of nonwhites lived in housing officially classified "substandard" by the Census Bureau. While the respective percentages dropped to 5 and 15 in 1966, the improvement did not overcome the growing proportion of central city housing classified as "deteriorating."

The fact is that many low- and moderate-income residents of the central cities cannot afford to pay the rent necessary to support decent housing. This not only prevents private builders from constructing new units, but also discourages them from maintaining structurally sound existing units, for either action involves an investment which cannot bring a fair return.

During the Kennedy-Johnson years, several important federal programs were enacted in the hope of inducing greater housing construction, especially for the poor living in central cities. Despite these programs, the over-all housing production rate between 1960 and 1968 averaged only 7.5 starts per thousand people, somewhat less than that of the Eisenhower years. Moreover, only 113,000 publicly-assisted housing starts were made in 1968; 51,000 in 1967, and 49,000 in 1966.[1]

Several factors act to dampen attempts to expand the construction of housing for low- and moderate-income persons, especially if units of this type are to be constructed in the suburbs: inadequate mortgage money, the backward state of housing technology, and restrictive local zoning regulations. Clearly, national and state action is needed if these problems are to be solved, but equally important are local initiative and area-wide coordination and planning. The present local governmental system makes local initiative nearly impossible and area-wide planning clearly impossible.

1/*New York Times*, March 16, 1969, Section 3, p. 1.

28.

Jobs and Training

The distribution of housing in metropolitan areas contributes substantially to the employment problems of many metropolitan area residents. The magnitude and dimensions of the unemployment problem in 1967 are summarized by the following findings of the U.S. Department of Labor:

- The approximately 450,000 unemployed persons in poverty neighborhoods were 15.3 per cent of the total unemployment in the nation, while their labor force was only 8.6 per cent of the nation's.

- The unemployment rate in poverty neighborhoods was 6.8 per cent in 1967, twice as high as the rate in the other urban neighborhoods and almost double the rate for the nation as a whole.

- Some 200,000 of the unemployed poverty residents were men and women in the prime working years, age 25 to 54. Teenagers (16 to 19) account for about 135,000; young workers (20 to 24), 75,000; and older workers (55 and over), 50,000.

- Of all the residents of poverty neighborhoods, blacks had the highest incidence of unemployment. The unemployment rate was 8.9 per cent for blacks and 5.3 per cent for whites.[1]

Among the causes of high unemployment rates in metropolitan poverty neighborhoods is an oversupply of unskilled labor. Victims of unemployment on the farms and in the mines, large numbers of men and women without vocational experience continue to migrate from rural to metropolitan areas at a rate too fast to be absorbed into the labor force.

Compounding the problem of oversupply is the mismatch in metropolitan areas between poverty neighborhoods and unskilled job opportunities. Due to their low incomes and/or racial discrimination, most unskilled workers are compelled to live in deteriorating areas of central cities at a time when the search for space, the demands of motor freight, the spread of external economies, and other factors are either

---

1/Paul M. Ryscavage and Hazel M. Willacy, "Employment of the Nation's Urban Poor," *Monthly Labor Review,* August 1968, pp. 15 and 16.

encouraging or facilitating the movement of blue-collar jobs from central cities to suburbs.*

Although some unskilled workers commute from their homes in the central cities to jobs in the suburbs, most cannot. Those who do often rely on public transportation, which, according to a U.S. Department of Labor survey, "is usually expensive, often circuitous, or simply not available."[1] In the New York metropolitan area, for example, it would cost a worker in Harlem about $40 a month to commute by public transportation to work in an aircraft plant in Farmingdale (Long Island), or in a parts plants in Yonkers or Port Chester (Westchester County).

While public programs could be designed to eliminate the mismatch between the location of poverty neighborhoods and unskilled job opportunities, they alone would not insure work for the group of metropolitan jobless commonly called "the hard-core unemployed." Always the first to be adversely affected by the slightest oversupply of unskilled workers, the hard-core unemployed have not developed the attitudes and basic work skills required for any but the most marginal jobs. Both at their own and the federal government's expense, a growing number of firms are developing on-the-job training programs which eventually may reduce significantly the number of hard-core unemployed in metropolitan poverty neighborhoods.

This Committee is currently investigating ways of eliminating poverty through jobs and training with a view to recommending a national policy in this field. Training programs—by whatever level of government—should strive to match job-seekers with jobs in each metropolitan area. Such a match will require metropolitan employment planning which must include training, housing, and transportation. Only metropolitan-wide planning is capable of producing this kind of interrelated program.

Transportation

Most of the transportation systems of metropolitan areas were built decades ago and remain fixed in the same place. From the largest to the smallest metropolitan area, the grid pattern street network re-

---

1/Dorothy K. Newman, "The Decentralization of Jobs," *Monthly Labor Review*, May 1967, p. 9.

*See Memorandum by MR. CHARLES KELLER, Jr., *page 60.*

mains as jammed in the twentieth century as it was in the nineteenth. While improvements in traffic engineering techniques, such as one-way streets and reversible street lanes, have speeded vehicular traffic slightly, delays are still the rule rather than the exception.

In the largest metropolitan areas especially, street traffic cannot be unknotted without large-scale construction of parking garages, basic changes in truck delivery schedules, and major investments in integrated systems of public transit. While the private automobile seems to be the cheapest and fastest means of personal transport in less populated sections of metropolitan areas, it is notoriously inefficient in central cities, particularly those with more than 750,000 in population. Yet it is unreasonable to expect travelers to use existing public transit facilities willingly in most central cities. Buses, which form the backbone of most public transit systems, are often old and uncomfortable, and are likely to follow inconvenient routes and schedules.

As metropolitan areas like San Francisco and Washington are now realizing, improving public transit in the central cities will by itself do little to upgrade metropolitan transportation. More and more, both central cities and suburbs are accepting the fact that traffic delays and congestion can be avoided only by bringing together and meshing the plans and policies of state highway departments, airport and bridge authorities, rapid transit authorities, bus companies, and all local governments.

Environmental Pollution

Like traffic congestion, environmental pollution has been a fact of American metropolitan life for years, but only recently, as it has grown worse, has the public begun to appreciate the dangers it holds in store for civilization's very existence. Traditionally, American urban dwellers have either ignored the pollution problem or attempted to solve it by forcing major institutional sources of pollution, mainly heavy industry, to move to the edge of their areas of settlement. Today, however, neither attitude is remotely reasonable.

Small-scale local governments are ill equipped either to prevent or to eliminate environmental pollution. In many metropolitan areas, the development of region-wide sewage disposal and pollution control authorities reflects popular realization of this fact. Too often, however, these authorities are given little in the way of preventive powers. They are mainly assigned the task of cleaning up existing problems.

Related to pollution are such matters as building codes, zoning restrictions, and transportation planning. Thus, it should be evident that the existing system of fragmented local government is a major impediment to the speedy elimination of environmental pollution.

$$* \quad * \quad *$$

The problems discussed here constitute only a few of the many problems of metropolitan America. Overcrowded public health facilities, physical ugliness, and inadequate recreation areas are others which limit the quality of metropolitan life.

To attack these problems requires adequate resources and a responsive governmental system. Further, the nature of a governmental system and its sources of revenue may themselves influence the nature of its problems and the likelihood of their solution. The need, therefore, is not only to examine the problems but, equally important, the resources and machinery available to solve them.

3.

Obstacles to the Solution
of Metropolitan Problems

Structural changes alone offer no panacea for the burgeoning problems of metropolitan areas. These problems cannot be solved without billions of dollars in additional expenditures, public and private. Despite the Vietnam War and an unyielding inflation, the nation has substantial financial resources—not enough to change conditions overnight but enough to make a significant start. Much more can be done to see that these resources are being used efficiently and effectively.

The cost to society of failing to spend the funds needed to solve our metropolitan problems is incalculable. Yet sufficient resources are not forthcoming at present for these important reasons: (1) the adverse attitudes of many taxpayers toward increased expenditures to pay for fundamental reforms; (2) the existing anti-urban biases of state and

33.

federal aid programs; (3) the imbalance between needs and resources created by the fragmented local government in metropolitan areas; and (4) the lack of vigorous state action.

Taxpayer Attitudes

Social critics have observed that many Americans are extremely reluctant to support government expenditures for any purpose. Rather than spend their money, through taxes, on improving society, they would prefer to make personal expenditures on consumer items as a means of improving their living standard.

This preference pattern is not solely the result of selfishness. It is also the outcome of a popular belief in the virtues of Jeffersonian government and self-help. Despite a generation of welfare democracy, a large number of Americans cling to the Jeffersonian view that "the only good government is small government." For diverse reasons, ranging from the philosophical to the most practical, these people simply do not believe that it is a responsibility of governments to undertake massive spending to solve social problems.

In metropolitan areas the complex interdependence of society dictates a larger role for government than was needed in a rural, small-town society. Traditional public functions such as education, police, sanitation, and transportation inevitably occupy a larger share of the total economy. New public problems and new concerns—and the failure of society to respond to them quickly enough—have widened the role of government still further. In order to cope successfully with these new problems, government must not only improve its own performance but encourage the private sector to respond as well. Private enterprise and individual initiative can make a major contribution to solving metropolitan problems but only in an atmosphere conducive to their employment. Government must play a role in creating that atmosphere.

To be sure, not all Americans oppose greatly expanded government expenditures on metropolitan problems. Growing numbers of persons—wealthy, middle-class, and poor alike—are becoming convinced that the nation must do more to satisfy current metropolitan needs. Jarred by massive civil disorders, these individuals are placing more and more pressure on civic officials to do something about the urban crisis.

Biases in Existing
Federal and State Aid Programs

The anti-central city, and to a lesser extent, the anti-metropolitan biases of existing state and federal aid programs demonstrate the need not only for more resources, but for a reallocation of those already being used. Today direct state and federal aid supports 27 per cent of all expenditures within central cities but 29 per cent of those in suburban areas and 37 per cent of all local expenditures in the remainder of the nation. If examined relative to local tax effort, direct federal and state aid is equivalent to only 44 per cent of central city taxes, while the comparable figures for suburbia and the rest of the nation are, respectively, 53 and 74 per cent.

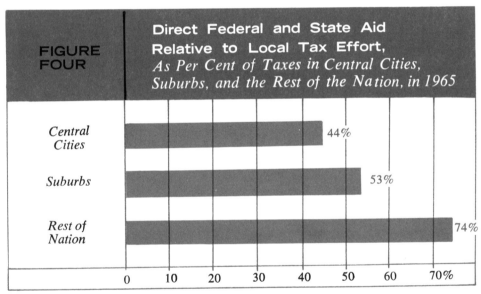

FIGURE FOUR

Direct Federal and State Aid Relative to Local Tax Effort, *As Per Cent of Taxes in Central Cities, Suburbs, and the Rest of the Nation, in 1965*

Central Cities — 44%
Suburbs — 53%
Rest of Nation — 74%

0 10 20 30 40 50 60 70%

Source: Advisory Commission on Intergovernmental Relations, *Fiscal Balance in the American Federal System,* Vol. 2 (Washington, D.C.: U.S. Government Printing Office, October 1967), p. 84.

It may well be that the single greatest failure of the aid system lies in education. Due to the workings of state education formulas, the amount of assistance, on the average, for suburban districts is substantially greater than that for city districts. Although current data is impossible to obtain, in 1962 per capita aid to education in the central city was $20.73, while in the suburban areas it was $37.66. On a per student basis the gap is even more striking. For example, in the year 1966-67 for New York State's six metropolitan areas, the average difference between educational aid to the central cities in those areas and to the school districts in the rest of the counties was $100 per pupil. For Albany, central city aid was $307 per pupil; for the rest of the county, $493. The comparable figures for the other areas are: Binghamton, $393 and $571; Buffalo, $351 and $425; Rochester, $297 and $453; Syracuse, $356 and $531. Aid to the school district of New York City was $319 per pupil while for the counties of Nassau, Rockland, Suffolk, and Westchester average aid was $453 per pupil.

Though some federal aid programs are still woefully inadequate, they reflect a considerably greater concern for metropolitan problems than do state aid programs. For education, job training, housing, and mass transit, for example, much more federal aid is forthcoming today than a decade ago.

A number of proposals have been made for strengthening fiscal relations among federal, state, and local governments. One is a plan for the federal government to provide unrestricted general assistance grants to states and localities. Another would provide a federal income tax reduction in the form of a partial tax credit, allowing individual taxpayers to offset a portion of their state income tax payments against their federal income tax liability. The tax credit proposal has been advanced by this Committee as an effective means of overcoming restraints on state taxation.[1]

Fragmented Local Units

Fragmented local government systems cannot deal effectively with existing metropolitan problems for reasons which we documented thoroughly in our earlier report on *Modernizing Local Government.*[2] But none is more important than their severe tax and expenditure disparities. Generally, local taxable resources are lacking in the very communities within metropolitan areas where the needs are most serious and more plentiful in places where they are least serious. As the Advisory Commission on Intergovernmental Relations has observed:

1/*A Fiscal Program for a Balanced Federalism,* a Statement on National Policy by the Research and Policy Committee, Committee for Economic Development, New York, June 1967, p. 49.

2/*Modernizing Local Government, op. cit.*

The large central cities are in the throes of a deepening fiscal crisis. On the one hand, they are confronted with the need to satisfy rapidly growing expenditure requirements triggered by the rising number of "high-cost" citizens. On the other hand, their tax resources are growing at a decreasing rate (and in some cases actually declining), a reflection of the exodus of middle and high income families and business firms from the central city to suburbia. . . .

Of growing significance are the fiscal disparities among rich and poor suburban communities in many of the metropolitan areas— disparities that often are even more dramatic than those observed between central cities and suburbia in general. Many of the older suburban communities are taking on the physical, social and economic characteristics of the central city. This type of community is especially vulnerable to fiscal distress because it lacks the diversified tax base that has enabled the central city to absorb some of the impact of extraordinary expenditure demands.[1]

The confused arrangement of local governments has also made it difficult for metropolitan areas to plan their physical and social development. As a consequence, growth has occurred in a disorderly and costly fashion.

Prior to 1966, federal aid programs mandated little in the way of metropolitan planning institutions. In general, they required only that all federally-assisted projects, such as airports and highways, conform to a comprehensive plan drawn up for the entire metropolitan community. However, beginning with the Housing and Urban Development Act of 1966, the federal government's planning requirements were broadened in scope. In Title II, Section 204, the Act specified that:

All applications made after June 30, 1967 for federal loans or grants to assist in carrying out open space land projects, or for the planning or construction of hospitals, airports, libraries, water supply distribution facilities, sewerage facilities and waste treatment works, highways, transportation facilities, and water de-

1/Advisory Commission on Intergovernmental Relations, *Fiscal Balance in the American Federal System,* Vol. 2 (Washington, D.C.: U.S. Government Printing Office, October 1967), pp. 5 and 6.

velopment and land conservation projects within any metropolitan area shall be submitted for review to any area-wide agency which is designated to perform metropolitan or regional planning for the area within which the assistance is to be used.[1]

This provision in the 1966 Housing and Urban Development Act culminated a long effort to encourage metropolitan-wide planning. Although the Act does not require the regional planning agency to approve a local jurisdiction's application for grants, it can comment unfavorably on it. When it does, the application goes back to the jurisdiction from which it originated. That jurisdiction may either change the application to meet the criticisms, or it may simply pass it on, with the unfavorable comments attached, to the appropriate agency in Washington.

According to the Act, the appropriate agency shall review the comments and recommendations "for the sole purpose of assisting it in determining whether the application is in accordance with the provisions of Federal law which govern the making of loans or grants." In other words, if there is no requirement for comprehensive planning in the specific federal grant program under which the local government is applying, the Washington agency has no legal power to consider the recommendations of the metropolitan planning agency. Even with this limitation, however, a power grant that could grow in significance is made by this Act to a new metropolitan jurisdiction which will compete for power with other units and, on occasion, will win.

It is not known, of course, what kind of policies such regional planning jurisdictions will adopt. Their significance, however, does not rest with the policies they adopt but rather with the fact that a jurisdiction with power to make such decisions has been created. Since this jurisdiction will be directly related to the programs of the federal government, it will have the power inherent in that relationship.

While increased metropolitan planning can minimize the long-run development of costly urban problems, it cannot be fully effective because of the present disarray of local governments. For this reason, many are suggesting that federal aid be used not only to push metropolitan planning but also to streamline the prevailing system of local government.

1/Housing and Urban Development Act of 1966, Title II, Section 204.

Role of the States

While there is support for federally-encouraged local government reorganization, the states are still considered the appropriate unit for tackling urban problems. The states have the necessary legal powers and access to sufficient resources. "But," as this Committee stated earlier, "few state governments have sought to collaborate with their major cities —or with other local units—in meeting critical local necessities."[1]

States could reorganize their local government systems, they could redirect their flow of aid, or they could assume directly the management of those public services having the greatest impact on their urban areas. One reason for the failure of the states to respond is clear. Except for New York, New Jersey, Connecticut, and California, no state has attempted to develop a comprehensive urban program, and even these states have had little success. No state has undertaken any massive program to improve its urban schools, to reduce welfare dependency, to plan comprehensive urban transportation systems, or to make the urban environment more livable.

Clearly, both structural and attitudinal factors prevent the marshalling of resources adequate to solve the nation's metropolitan problems. Moreover, these two sets of factors are interlocking. One reinforces the other. Existing governmental and fiscal structures result in institutional advantages for some communities and disadvantages for others. These advantages and disadvantages, in turn, encourage attitudes which support both maintenance of and resistance to change of existing structures.

Strong attachments to local communities, especially in the suburbs, make it enormously difficult to reform local government in metropolitan areas, to bring about changes in the federal and state-local aid systems, and to institute new programs capable of meeting the nation's most pressing urban needs, especially those in the central cities. Nonetheless, massive urban civil disorders, incipient taxpayer revolts, and the injustice of existing governmental and fiscal structures make such reforms and innovations imperative.

1/*Modernizing State Government*, a Statement on National Policy by the Research and Policy Committee, Committee for Economic Development, New York, July 1967, p. 11.

39.

4. Reshaping Metropolitan Government

Today's metropolitan problems are not all permanent. Continuing change in the structure and behavior of metropolitan society will cause some problems to disappear while others will persist and be joined by problems yet unforeseen.

To meet existing metropolitan problems as well as to anticipate future ones, the United States must develop governmental institutions, instruments, and programs which are more consistent, responsive, and flexible. It must go beyond reorganizing central city and suburban government, beyond overhauling the federal and state-local fiscal system, beyond developing packages of new substantive programs. It must do all of these things and at the same time coordinate its efforts with an over-all national metropolitan policy.

40.

Improving Governmental Machinery

Central to the solution of the nation's greatest urban problems is the creation of improved governmental machinery in metropolitan areas. Better machinery will not by itself guarantee the development and adoption of more effective substantive programs, but it is a necessary prerequisite. Nor will the reform of governmental organizations guarantee the massive supply of resources essential to solving metropolitan problems. It could, however, aid in marshalling those resources as well as contributing to their effective allocation and utilization.

Aware of the need for change, enlightened business and civic leaders in metropolitan areas have spearheaded campaigns to replace small-scale, overlapping local governments with consolidated, federated, or other forms of metropolitan government. These campaigns have stressed the fact that the economic and social interdependence of metropolitan areas has created problems which can only be solved on an area-wide basis. Such citizen efforts have produced scattered results. In 1962 the City of Nashville, Tennessee, consolidated with Davidson County to form Metropolitan Nashville-Davidson County, a single metropolitan government. In 1968, the City of Jacksonville, Florida, joined with Duval County in a similar move.* Area-wide jurisdictions with lesser degrees of consolidation have also been set up in metropolitan Miami, Baton Rouge, Seattle, Portland, and Indianapolis.**

Outside the United States there has been another development. In 1954 the Province of Ontario, Canada, established a new 241-square mile Municipality of Metropolitan Toronto, a federation of local governments with functions shared by two levels of government—one area-wide and one local. This form of metropolitan government is similar to what we are recommending in this statement. A description of Toronto's government appears in Appendix B.

Despite the dedicated efforts of many proponents of good government, opposition to the concept of a common governmental jurisdiction for metropolitan areas in the United States remains fierce. Many explanations have been offered as to why voters and public officials fail to endorse metropolitan government—fear of "Big Government," higher taxes, or a loss of political power; sheer resistance to change; or simply a lack of information. All of these factors undoubtedly come into play.

---

*See Memorandum by MR. CHARLES P. TAFT, *page 60.*
**See Memorandum by MR. CHARLES KELLER, Jr., *page 60.*

41.

Citizens of metropolitan areas represent communities with diverse characteristics, tax resources, and viewpoints, which are not easily changed for the sake of area-wide solutions.

Increasing Intergovernmental Cooperation

Advocates of area-wide government are convinced that the changes they seek will some day materialize, if not in the fashion or at the speed they once expected. Several developments support their optimism: (1) federal assistance for the rapidly growing number of metropolitan councils of government and metropolitan regional planning agencies; (2) growing use of county home rule charters in single-county metropolitan areas; (3) adoption by many urban counties of executive-headed governments; (4) interagency—city, state, and federal—coordination through such programs as model cities; and (5) increasing intergovernmental cooperation.

Expanding intergovernmental cooperation within metropolitan areas has taken many forms, ranging from informal agreements among government officials of adjoining jurisdictions to the much more fundamental act of establishing metropolitan or nearly metropolitan-wide special districts for the performance of single functions. To date, however, intergovernmental cooperation has not reduced the number of local non-school jurisdictions in metropolitan areas. In 1962 there were 14,745 non-school governments in America's 212 metropolitan areas; in 1967, there were 15,684 in the same places, an increase of 6.4 per cent. The increase has been primarily in one-function special districts—units spawned by the inadequacies of traditional governments.

Area-Wide Government or Community Control?

Steps in the direction of area-wide government are not surprising when considered in their historical context. For nearly two centuries, American government has become increasingly centralized. Cities have expanded their boundaries by annexation. States have assumed new functions or have taken more responsibility for old ones. The national government has broadened its role in domestic affairs. Traditionally, much support for centralization has been based on the assumption that it leads to better, more responsive government and more humane social policies.

It may seem paradoxical, therefore, that today's growing support for decentralization of big city government should rest upon the same assumption. Advocates of decentralization see it as an effective means of involving members of the community in the governmental process—giving them more access to public services and more control over the government bureaucracy.

Backers of centralization, on the other hand, contend that only a larger governmental unit can achieve economies of scale and make maximum use of fiscal resources and new technologies, and for these reasons it can be more responsive to the growing needs of its citizens, the disadvantaged particularly.

It is clear from the foregoing that what is needed is a system of government that adequately recognizes *both* forces, centralization and decentralization. Such a system must permit a genuine sharing of power over functions between a larger unit and a smaller unit. It must recognize a larger unit to permit economies of scale, area-wide planning, and equities in finance. It must recognize a smaller unit to permit the exercise of local power over matters which affect the lives of local citizens.

Combining Centralization and Decentralization

All metropolitan areas are affected to a greater or lesser extent by the conflicting forces of centralization and decentralization. The interdependence of activities within metropolitan areas requires area-wide institutions for some functions or parts of functions of government. Just as clear is the need for units of government small enough to enable the recipients of government services to have some voice and control over their quality and quantity.

The usual result of this conclusion is to try to divide functions, assigning some to a more general level of government and others to the local level. However, the American federal system permits a much wider choice than such a clear-cut division would imply. Federalism has, in fact, undergone continuous change and the division of responsibility among levels of government has become much less distinct. Instead of dividing functions, the practice has been that different parts of the federal

43.

system perform different aspects of the same function. Financing may be assigned to one part of this system, while administration is assigned to another. Seldom is it even this neat. Policy-making, administrative, and fiscal responsibilities for the same function may be divided in a great variety of combinations among all parts of the system. The result is a sharing of power over functions rather than a division of functions.

While the American federal system has been dividing responsibility and power among many layers of government, the gradual evolution of an American administrative doctrine has produced a set of theories and practices that tend to reduce citizen influence on many aspects of government. In part a result of the reform movement of the 1920's and 1930's, these practices were primarily designed to increase efficiency and to reduce political influence. However, concepts about separation of policy and administration, about professionalism and hierarchical control have all worked in the direction of excluding the average citizen from participation in the delivery of government services.

The kind of participation encouraged has been only at the policy-making level, where blue-ribbon citizens advisory committees are frequently employed. But below this level administrative expertise is supposed to take over. The parent of the public school child, the welfare recipient, the hospital patient, and all others whose lives are affected by government are supposed to accept as final the decisions of professional "experts." Citizens with greater political weight normally ignore these claims to expertise and effectively influence the operation of the system, be it a school system or some other public activity. Citizens with less influence—and those lacking sophistication in dealing with the political process—find it more difficult to gain access to the system.

It is in part the frustrations produced by this administrative ideology that have led to demands for decentralization and community control. For the average citizen, exerting an influence on the delivery of services is much more important than making a vague, distant impact on high-level policy deliberations.

Two Levels of Government

In principle a governmental system for America's metropolitan areas must recognize the need for both a community level and a metropolitan level of government. There are many different governmental arrangements that will meet this need. As long as legitimate demands for centralization and decentralization are met, the specific arrangements may vary to fit the economic, cultural, and political characteristics of each area. Some may require greater emphasis on consolidation of local units; others may require greater emphasis on creating units which will enhance community participation.

Therefore, in the following proposals to achieve the dual advantages of a combined community-metropolitan governmental system, we would expect variations in application. In some cases a comprehensive solution may be feasible at an early date. In other areas achievement of an effective two-level system may require several steps over a period of time.

To gain the advantages of both centralization and decentralization, we recommend as an ultimate solution a governmental system of two levels. Some functions should be assigned in their entirety to the area-wide government, others to the local level, but most will be assigned in part to each level.* More important than the division of functions is the *sharing of power*. Local communities will be assigned some power over functions placed at the area-wide level of government. Further, state and federal governments must be involved in most functions. This two-level system will not provide neatness and symmetry, but effectiveness, responsiveness, and adequate resources.

In those situations where the metropolitan area is contained within one county, a reconstituted county government should be used as the basic framework for a new area-wide government. This may, but need not, include consolidation of a large dominant central city with the county government in which it is located. If there are two or more sizable cities in the county, consolidation may not be appropriate. Counties in some states already have very wide powers. An indispensable requirement is the restructuring of such counties with a suitable legislative organ, a strong chief executive, and modern management.

In cases where the metropolitan area spreads over several counties or towns, a new jurisdiction should be created which embraces all of its territory. Although a federation of existing counties and towns might be considerably easier to implement, it is clear that rapid metropolitan growth makes a stronger jurisdiction considerably more appropriate, especially for purposes of long-range planning.

Most complicated is the interstate metropolitan area. Since state government has primary responsibility for local government organiza-

---

*See Memorandum by MR. HERMAN L. WEISS, *page 59.*

45.

tion, an area-wide metropolitan government crossing state lines would require close harmony between or among the states involved. Exact uniformity of the units on both sides of the line would be impossible, but by agreement or compact the states could design a system which would mesh. Two units, one on each side of the state line, would find it far easier to work out agreements for area-wide action than the present dozens of such units. Interstate agreements have created single-function units which operate in more than one state. Similar arrangements for a multi-function unit certainly should not be beyond the ingenuity of man.*

In addition to an area-wide level, modern metropolitan government should contain a community-level government system comprised of "community districts." These units might consist of existing local governments with functions readjusted to the two-level system, together with new districts in areas where no local unit exists. The new community districts should not be imposed from without, but created through local initiative by the simplest possible methods. A state boundary commission or similar body might be established to begin the process of delineating new districts. Citizen groups which seek community-district status might first make their appeal to this body if it is established.

In some cities there are areas which already possess strong community identity and these could become the new community districts. But in many cities, particularly the big cities, the sense of community is diminishing. Isolation and alienation, on the other hand, are increasing. Once the smaller political units are created—units with genuine power—a stronger sense of community is bound to emerge. In the suburbs, existing municipalities are likely to be retained as the community districts. Except in the most recently settled suburbs, these municipalities tend not only to represent "natural areas," but also to have well-developed community identities. Thus, local communities in both cities and suburbs can be guaranteed full participation within the metropolitan system.

Size and Representation

A major difficulty in establishing community districts will be determining their size. Although much of the literature on government organization places heavy emphasis on appropriate size of minor jurisdic-

---

*See Memorandum by MR. CHARLES P. TAFT, *page 60.*

tions, the fact is there is little hard economic evidence of what the optimum size should be. Therefore, how a community perceives its identity becomes important as well as the number of people it contains.

States should establish suggested, but not mandatory, criteria to guide the actual determination of community boundaries. The states should, in addition, set down requirements which will guarantee the representativeness of the government established. Although the community districts should be allowed to determine their form of government—council, strong executive, commission, or some other form—the basic requirement of one-man, one-vote should be met.*

State governments should assist the organization of community districts by enacting enabling legislation to permit the creation of a two-level form of metropolitan government and by establishing a procedure through which community districts may be created. Great flexibility as to size and governmental organization should be permitted.

The states should also prescribe guidelines for determining size and representation of the area-wide government. The practice exists in some metropolitan areas of representing community units—towns and villages—on an area-wide governing council. However, this form of representation rarely produces an area-wide point of view but rather a bargaining process through which the various smaller units try to protect their parochial interests. Therefore, we suggest that delegates to the area-wide government represent legislative districts on a one-man, one-vote basis instead of representing the community districts as such.

It is important to underline the full significance of the changes advocated here. **City boundaries would become less important than they now are. There would be a boundary surrounding each metropolitan area as well as boundaries surrounding community districts within each metropolitan area.**

Relating Area-Wide
and Community Responsibilities

More difficult than determining community size and governmental system is establishing community administrative, fiscal, and policy responsibilities vis-à-vis the area-wide level of metropolitan government.

---

*See Memorandum by MR. ROBERT R. NATHAN, *page 59.*

To assist this process, states must specify criteria which will insure the following: (1) high levels of local community initiative; (2) adequate performance of all public service functions; (3) equitable distribution of the burdens and benefits of the metropolitan fiscal base; (4) satisfactory resolution of political conflicts; and (5) greater flexibility in anticipating and responding to the gamut of metropolitan problems.

If these results are to be guaranteed, some functions must be assigned entirely to the area-wide government, with the participation of local communities limited to hearings, powers of delay, and in some cases the right of veto. And, some functions must be delegated completely to the local communities. Where circumstances permit, local communities should be given the option of performing still other functions, but according to guidelines specified by the area-wide government.

State and Federal Aid

No government organization can make a major contribution to the solution of America's urban ills without adequate funding to carry out substantive programs. Such funding will require greater contributions from all parts of the governmental system.

Reorganization of government in metropolitan areas will make it possible to increase over-all fiscal resources. America's wealth is concentrated largely in its metropolitan areas and metropolitan-wide government is advocated, in part, so this resource base may be preserved and improved. The existing system of overlapping local governments results in a poor match between needs and resources and perpetuates waste, inefficiency, and confusion.

Since the community districts will vary greatly in size and resources, the bulk of their financing will be through grants-in-aid or shared taxes that come from the metropolitan level of government, the state, and the federal government. To the extent that locally-raised revenues will be employed, they will be raised principally through the property tax, the only tax appropriate for a jurisdiction of the size contemplated. Fees and charges may also be employed by this local level.

Most important will be the new revenue sources available to the metropolitan-wide level. By encompassing an entire area that is economically and socially interdependent, this level will have at its disposal revenues available from sources other than the property tax. Moreover,

48.

the distortion produced by present competitive tax behavior within metro-politan areas will be substantially reduced.

Although the establishment of metropolitan-wide government will make possible a greater fiscal contribution, it will by no means eliminate the need for substantial state and federal aid. **There is urgent need for a greater and more equitable state aid contribution and more attention by the states to the adequacy of their local governmental systems.** The states have responsibilities for their local governmental systems. They should adapt their aid systems to the facts of metropolitanism and adjust the boundaries of local governments to fit current realities. In *A Fiscal Program for a Balanced Federalism*, we stated:

> *Because of the increasing interdependence of local jurisdictions, the role of the states must grow if they are to be strong and effective partners in the federal system. The states should encourage greater cooperation and coordination among local governments in solving metropolitan problems. In many areas taxpaying ability is greatest in the suburbs but needs are greatest in the central cities. The states should do more to equalize resources available to individual local governments to combat social ills.*[1]

The powers and responsibilities of the states have been exercised sparingly, if at all. As we have already explained, the state aid system is designed particularly to aid suburban areas, creating far higher tax burdens in cities than in most suburban communities. The earlier bias of state legislatures for the rural areas has been translated by reapportionment into a bias in favor of suburban areas. There was a time when such rural bias was justified by the distribution of taxable resources. The wealth of the country was concentrated in the urban areas, and if minimum levels of government service were to be maintained in rural areas, aid was necessary. However, the redistribution of taxable resources within metropolitan areas between central cities and their suburbs does not justify the current suburban preference.

The states have the power to assume functions that are now performed locally, but few have assumed them. In some states, highways and welfare have become a major state responsibility, and a few municipal higher educational institutions have been taken over by the states. But

---

1/*A Fiscal Program for a Balanced Federalism, op. cit.,* p. 30.

there has been no major shift in functions to ease local fiscal burdens.

Although states have passed permissive legislation making inter-local cooperation possible, they have not undertaken any major overhaul of local government. This is in direct contrast to the Canadian provinces which have actually established metropolitan governments for some of their cities.[1]

The response of the federal government to local fiscal problems has been more positive. The federal aid system, for example, through such programs as urban renewal, aid to education, and the anti-poverty program, is adjusting its assistance programs to the problems of the cities. It is possible that by giving more attention to the flow of aid the federal government will be able to help fill the gap left by the state aid system.

Both state and federal aid systems should be restructured in order to put resources where they are most needed. Equally important, state and federal aid should be used to stimulate government reorganization. The use of aid for this purpose has a precedent in its use in promoting school consolidation by the states. **Therefore, we recommend that state and federal aid should be used as an incentive to promote the kind of restructured government outlined in this statement.**

Restructuring central city and suburban government and revising the existing federal and state aid systems will greatly alleviate many existing metropolitan problems. However, the complexity of the problems themselves makes it doubtful that they can be solved adequately without a battery of new or modified substantive programs.

There is, at present, no lack of programs proposed to solve the nation's metropolitan problems. While many are praiseworthy, few have been designed as parts of rationally integrated packages. Consequently, they are often overlapping and flatly contradictory. When implemented in highly interdependent metropolitan areas, their consequences are often exceptionally perverse.

A reorganized local government system, therefore, can play a major role in making substantive programs relevant to the problems of metropolitan areas. Such a revised local system could give new vitality to America's traditional federalism by forcing the state and federal parts of the system to design programs which are internally consistent and genuinely responsive to the needs of its urban citizens.

1/See Appendix B.

50.

Sharing Power Over Functions

Despite differences from metropolitan area to metropolitan area, and from state to state, it is possible to outline some basic arrangements for sharing responsibilities for individual functions between area-wide governments and community districts. While the following breakdown of tasks must surely be modified to meet the peculiar needs of each metropolitan area, it does illustrate the kinds of division broadly necessary to insure workable two-level metropolitan government.

Planning. An obvious function for assignment to the area-wide government is planning. While the federal government is encouraging the establishment of metropolitan planning agencies, these units lack the power necessary to guide area-wide development effectively. Increasingly, they must be given greater control over the provision of transportation facilities, sewage disposal, water supply, and recreation areas.

Planning agencies, however, should not be given complete control over the zoning process; there must be a division of this responsibility. Community districts must have some say over zoning if they are to control their own character, but they must not allow zoning to become an institutional block against minority groups. In general, the metropolitan-wide level should be empowered to specify broad areas of industrial, commercial, and residential activity which the local communities could zone into smaller sub-areas.

Community districts, however, must have a role in the area-wide planning process which extends beyond zoning. To insure effective participation in this process, the community governments must establish their own planning agencies. These agencies should be empowered not only to develop social and physical plans for their own areas, but also to inspect and, if necessary, to delay plans designed by the area-wide government. Correspondingly, the area-wide government must be given the prerogative to veto any community plans that do not serve the interest of the entire metropolitan area—a right not possessed by the metropolitan planning agencies set up under the 1966 Housing and Urban Development Act.

Transportation. This function must be assigned in large part to the metropolitan-wide unit because of its significance to the development of the entire area. However, the federal and state governments must assume greater responsibility for designing and financing comprehensive transportation policies. By its very nature, transportation cannot be planned solely on an intra-metropolitan basis. Fortunately, in this regard, the Nixon Administration has announced its intention to develop a federal transportation policy which not only will assign priorities among modes of transportation but also will design an aid system which reflects these priorities.

Because of its importance to community development, the formulation of area-wide transportation policies must involve community participation, for metropolitan transportation systems must facilitate the journey to work, expedite the shipment of goods, and speed the flow of traffic without adversely affecting local residents. The more than 20 interstate expressway controversies now raging indicate the degree to which highway plans can upset neighborhoods and communities. Current federal regulations requiring two hearings well in advance of interstate highway land acquisitions are a meaningful step in the direction of community participation. They must be strengthened, however, by provisions mandating community involvement in the over-all highway planning process.

Water Supply and Sewage Disposal. By their very nature, water supply and sewage disposal, like transportation, are area-wide functions. But unlike transportation, they do not require much local participation. Any number of arrangements can be employed to provide water and sewage disposal on an area-wide basis. In the case of sewage, the area-wide government can either build and manage the entire system for itself or assign the construction and management of feeder lines, but not trunks, to the local communities.

Rubbish and Garbage Collection. Unlike the sanitation functions discussed above, rubbish and garbage collection may be performed wholly at the local level. The level of service, such as frequency of pick-ups, can and should be left to community determination. The area-wide government's only control over this function should be one of policing—insuring that community performance meets specified limits of environmental pollution.*

Education. Currently, many large city governments are weighing responses to increasingly insistent demands for greater community control over public education. These demands inevitably revolve about the

---

*See Memorandum by MR. CHARLES P. TAFT, *page 61.*

conclusion that the schools—particularly those in ghetto areas—have failed.

Although community control of education has been widely discussed, the idea implies different things to different communities. In suburban communities, for example, it entails local financing. In ghetto districts it does not, for this would result in confiscatory tax rates or in the allocation of very few resources to education.

While some advocates of community control favor metropolitan or even state-wide financing of education, they often disagree sharply over what parts of the education function should be performed or controlled at the local level. In the coming months, a CED policy statement on educating the disadvantaged will discuss community responsibilities for education in poor areas.

Welfare. Were there not changes contemplated in forms of federal and state welfare support, fiscal realities would dictate that the function at the very least be financed on a metropolitan-wide basis. However, the current discussion over welfare financing has produced strong pressures for a substantially higher proportion of financing at the federal level, which would relieve lower levels of a heavy burden.

The movement of this function to a higher level of government could also increase administrative flexibility. Therefore, in order to guarantee protection of the welfare recipients' rights, the community-level government could play an important role. Since the financing of welfare is likely to be and should be at higher levels in the system, the Department of Welfare at the community level could become the advocate of those welfare recipients who believe they are not being properly treated by the system. Such a local welfare department would also be in a better position to provide services beyond the monthly welfare check.

Public Health. Like most functions of government, public health is really a group of functions, closely related but distinct in their activities. Public health is normally divided into: (1) environmental sanitation; (2) control of communicable disease; (3) vital statistics; (4) maternal and child health services; (5) laboratories; and (6) health education. Environmental sanitation, communicable disease control, and statistics should be administered metropolitan-wide with state and federal governments having clear responsibilities for establishing standards, while the other activities may be handled locally and merely coordinated by the area-wide agency.

Public health offices should be located in each community with the local community government participating in the operation of these decentralized offices. In fact, health centers should be combined with those other facilities which provide non-health social services.

The provision of hospital and other medical care facilities is more complex than public health because of the mixture of public and private roles in these services. Public hospital services are now supplied by counties and cities and special hospital districts covering several municipalities. Hospital services in addition are often purchased from privately operated hospitals by local governments for indigent patients.

There is a growing demand from many citizens—although not as insistent as with education—for more community control over their hospitals. Service levels are often considered too low and, for residents of ghetto neighborhoods particularly, such services are often inaccessible.

Adequate hospital and medical care is a national problem. Area-wide governments are appropriate units for planning for the provision of such care facilities within state and national guidelines. But there must be a role in the governance of such facilities which includes places for community residents on their governing boards.*

Housing. Related to education, welfare, and health is the provision of adequate housing. Probably no activity of government more clearly demonstrates the conflict between area-wide needs and community self-interest. Central city communities and suburban municipalities alike have bitterly opposed the placement of public housing within their boundaries.

Although housing is primarily the responsibility of private industry, to the extent that industry does not meet the needs of lower-income groups governmental subsidies are necessary. It is the public housing resulting from these subsidized programs which is opposed in many communities. The result is the concentration of such housing in ghetto areas, thereby eliminating the possible advantage of locating it in surroundings which would improve the total living environment of its residents.

Further, the location of subsidized housing in ghettos is inconsistent with the location of jobs which the residents of this housing might hold. There is obviously a need for scattered-site public housing, for rent subsidies, and for home ownership through interest-rate subsidy. Pro-

---

*See Memorandum by MR. MARION B. FOLSOM, *page 61*.

grams to provide all of these and other types of subsidized housing are on the federal statute books. All are underfunded, if funded at all.

Once the federal government puts housing policy in order and provides the necessary financing, the roles of metropolitan-wide and community governments must be fit into the system. There is a need for metropolitan-wide housing plans which include the deconcentration of subsidized housing. In fact, such metropolitan-wide plans should include the development of new towns—both inside and outside the cities—which contain populations that are balanced in terms of income and race. The type of governmental system recommended here will encourage this kind of development. At the community level, authority should be granted for participation in the planning of housing and for a role in the management of housing programs. Within large scale projects, resident participation is necessary.

Publicly subsidized renewal is probably even more related to the local community than housing. In fact, the kind of community governments recommended will provide a useful framework for urban renewal activities. Although it will be necessary for the area-wide agency to design broad outlines of urban renewal policy for the region, these area-wide plans will be in large part the sum of individual community plans.

Current model cities legislation provides the framework for the development of genuine community government incorporating not only renewal but all the other federal, state, and local programs designed to improve and reshape neighborhoods. The community districts suggested here are consistent with the original concept of model cities and seem more sound than recently announced plans to make the program applicable to the whole city.

Police. A two-level governmental system provides the opportunity for genuine reform of what may be the most sensitive of all public services. Parts of the police function must be area-wide—laboratories, communications systems, records systems, detective services, and inspection—if the police function is to be adequately performed. On the other hand, patrol services should probably be decentralized and under some community control.

At least one major metropolitan county—Nassau County in New York State—has demonstrated how this can be done. In that county of 1.5 million people, there is a county-wide police service covering police activities that must be area-wide. Many local communities within the county provide their own patrol services through local police depart-

55.

ments or buy a county patrol service. The citizen of Nassau pays two police taxes—one to the county for the centralized services and another to either the village government which provides that service or to the county for district police services.

Since the citizen has his most direct and frequent contact with the patrolman, it is the patrol function which is most sensitive. Community participation in this aspect of police service will inspire greater confidence between citizen and police.

Other Functions. Although other substantive functions could be covered, the basic pattern of assignment contemplated is illustrated by those already discussed. Of greatest importance is the fact that no hard lines have been drawn between functions or even parts of functions or between levels of government. The emphasis is on the *sharing of power and responsibility* and not on the assignment of entire functions to either level.

The recommendations contained in this statement recognize two preconditions for a revitalized metropolitan America—the need for jurisdictions large enough to cope with problems that pervade entire areas, and, at the same time, the need for jurisdictions small enough to allow citizens to take part—and take pride—in the process of government. Our guidelines are neither simple nor perfect. The complex pressures and counterpressures of metropolis cannot be contained by any easy, all-purpose blueprint. However, we believe that the proposals we have outlined provide the foundation upon which concerned citizens may build a better metropolitan government suited to their needs.

Memoranda of Comment,
Reservation, or Dissent

Page 10—By ALLAN SPROUL:

I must again record the view that the thrust of CED Statements can be diluted or become lost in an excess of verbiage which darts into by-ways of discussion, indulges in extended references to previous Policy Statements on the same general subject, and acquires the character of a term paper rather than a call to action by a group of businessmen.

The need for improvement in the structure and organization of government in metropolitan America is no longer a matter which requires educational tracts. The problem is one of ways and means of untangling the present tangle of local governments. Action has most often stumbled over the difficulty of modifying existing forms of government so as to approach a solution of area problems without destroying the identities of established communities.

This Policy Statement suggests an approach—a governmental system at two levels—which has a rational basis and which has achieved a large measure of success when tried in a Canadian metropolitan area. The Statement should be not only addressed to "concerned citizens," but to the governments of the several States, and should recommend that they provide the political leadership which is essential if there is to be effective consideration of this approach to the problem, as adapted to the needs of metropolitan areas in their jurisdictions.

Page 18—By PHILIP SPORN, with which FRAZAR B. WILDE has asked to be associated:

The meat of the coconut of this report is in this summary, which outlines a series of political solutions in the form of highly involved governmental reorganizations for what is a complex, most difficult, and potentially tragic development in national population movement that has brought about almost unbearable economic pressures on most of our great northern cities.

The report having failed to recognize the basic cause of the trouble and its locus, I cannot approve the main recommendations. They simply do not go far or deep enough.

It is not the cities and suburbs that are in trouble. It is mainly the cities such as New York, Washington, Chicago, Philadelphia, Newark, Cleveland, Detroit, Los Angeles, that are in trouble and not so much because of the departure of business firms and white residents but because of the exodus of large blocks of our underprivileged population, mostly black, from the south in their search for a more decent life. Thus, while the country's population increased 18.5% between 1950 and 1960 and that of New York City in the same period was static, the Negro population of California, New York, Pennsylvania, Illinois, Washington, D.C., Michigan, Ohio, increased 57%. Most of them settled in the great cities. This shift in city black population was at a rate two and a half times as fast as the shift in agricultural population that took place in the period 1925-1966.

This rapid, high intensity shift brought with it an extension of the life, and the worsening of the condition, of our slums, much greater loads on welfare and relief programs, much more pressing problems on the educational facilities, increases in the character and extent of violence, greater burdens on over-extended transportation facilities, and a general decline in the ability of our cities to handle these difficult problems.

Since this is a part of a great and inescapable national adjustment in population, it is obvious that the resulting heavy burden should be placed where it belongs—on the national shoulders. The necessary solutions are well beyond the scope of this note of comment. It is inconceivable to me, however, that it can be effected without major commitments to an equalization program between the states in such areas as relief and welfare payments, educational opportunities, minimum wage standards, employment opportunities, and related basic social-economic factors that affect the quality and standard of living, particularly in the lower economic brackets where too large a percentage of our black population finds itself.

Pages 19 and 45—By HERMAN L. WEISS:

This principal recommendation of the report is both necessary and valid for now. But predicated as it is on Standard Metropolitan Statistical Areas, it raises the question whether SMSA's are the most appropriate units of governmental size and scope for the long run. Current population and land development trends are generating only a very limited number of super-metropoli in this country, like the Boston-to-Washington, Pittsburgh-to-Cleveland and San Francisco-to-San Jose megalopoli. This fact, coupled with the difficulties of developing metropolitan governments that cross state boundaries, suggests that we may have to take a new look at this whole question, with special reference to how our historic federal system can, if it can, accommodate to these national growth and population patterns. As this report suggests, though, we must walk before we run.

Pages 21 and 47—By ROBERT R. NATHAN:

Some minimum size for local communities must be made mandatory. It is desirable to group people within boundaries in order to reflect common views and common functions. However, there is danger of breaking down local community governmental units into segments which are so minute as to make even more rigid the lines of demarcation and the divisions between groups with divergent attitudes and interests. Our society benefits from diverging as well as from converging interests. We certainly do not want to encourage polarization through a multiplicity of ineffective though largely homogeneous governmental entities.

In this process of change and adjustment of powers and functions serious consideration should be given at the community-level governmental system to consolidate or even divide present cities and towns and other local governments. Time of change affords an excellent opportunity to eliminate excessive and overlapping jurisdictions where they are not essential for effective local power and for needed changes in local boundaries. Flexibility is needed and should be encouraged in order to achieve both responsive and responsible local governing units.

Page 30—By CHARLES KELLER, JR.:

I think this statement should be restricted to such jobs in manufacturing and distribution, since blue collar jobs in the cities related to the service industries and construction are not, I believe, moving to the suburbs.

Page 41—By CHARLES P. TAFT:

I have been informed that one of the reasons for the voter support of Metro in Nashville and Jacksonville was the fear that within the existing city boundaries the black voter would take over. The absorption of the core city in the County insured, the citizens felt, the continuance of white domination of the community as a whole. This perhaps should have been explored. If true it might happen elsewhere.

Page 41—By CHARLES KELLER, JR.:

The City of New Orleans has had jurisdiction for all the functions it performs over the entire parish (county) of Orleans for many years. Functions now performed by other single purpose entities within the area might well be consolidated with the City of New Orleans.

Page 46—By CHARLES P. TAFT:

The recommendation as to the interstate metropolitan area is theoretically sound. In fact, however, two elements may slow it down drastically. The state may be so incompetent in the area of interstate compacts that it takes forever, to get any area-wide governmental form, over the fierce opposition the paper describes so vividly. Secondly, the underlying opposition to certain reforms (industrial opposition) to air pollution control joins natural incompetence and slow processing both under the governor and under the state legislature that the frustrated citizenry finds no point to apply pressure. There should be an intermediate step permitted—organization of interstate activity under home rule powers, with submission then to the legislature and to the U. S. Congress for ratification.

Page 52—By CHARLES P. TAFT:

I disagree wholly with the paragraph on Rubbish and Garbage Collection. It has now become clear that in real metropolitan areas the landfill method becomes impossible. The incinerator process has to grow so fast, and has to absorb very difficult plastic container materials that the expense is growing with the pressure of demand. The only hopeful solution is the compression process forming cubes to be shipped to abandoned quarries and closed mines. The cost is less than two fifths of the incineration process. Cincinnati will begin on this in 1970.

Page 54—By MARION B. FOLSOM:

In recent years, many communities have established health planning councils to plan and coordinate health facilities and services, both public and private.

Under Public Law 89-749 (Comprehensive Health Planning Law) Federal funds are available on a matching basis for Comprehensive Health Planning Councils at the State, regional and local levels.

Public Health officials should participate actively in the organization and functioning of widely representative councils, designed to expand and improve the quality and effectiveness of health care.

Appendices:

Metropolitanism

THE STANDARD METROPOLITAN STATISTICAL AREA (SMSA)

I. DEFINITION

Except in New England, a standard metropolitan statistical area is a county or group of contiguous counties which contain at least one city of 50,000 inhabitants or more, or "twin cities" with a combined population of at least 50,000.

In addition to the county, or counties, containing a central city or cities, contiguous counties are included in an SMSA if, according to certain criteria, they are essentially metropolitan in character and are socially and economically integrated with the central city.

In New England, SMSA's consist of towns and cities, rather than counties.

Source: U.S. Bureau of the Census, *Statistical Abstract of the United States: 1969* (90th Edition), Washington, D.C., 1969.

63.

II. NUMBER AND COMPOSITION OF SMSA'S

(a) Number

1953	170
1960	189
1967	228
1969	233

(b) Composition of SMSA'S, 1967

One county SMSA's	*123*
Two county SMSA's	*49*
Three county SMSA's	*27*
Four county SMSA's	*14*
Five or more county SMSA's	*15*
	Total 228

Source: The National Commission on Urban Problems, *Government Structure, Finance and Taxation,* Part IV, Washington, D.C., 1969.

III. EXTENT

(a) The great majority of the U.S. population lives in metropolitan areas. In 1966 more than two-thirds of the U.S. population was concentrated in 455 metropolitan counties. The remaining one-third of the population was scattered throughout the more than 2,600 remaining counties.

SMSA Population as Per Cent of Total Population 1900-1985

1900	41.9%
1910	45.7
1920	49.7
1930	54.3
1940	55.1
1950	59.0
1960	63.0
1965	64.4
1985 *(projected)*	71.0

Source: U.S. Bureau of the Census, *Population Estimates and Projections: Estimates of the Population of Counties in Metropolitan Areas, July 1, 1966, a Summary Report.* Series P-25, No. 427, Washington, D.C., July 31, 1969.

IV. GROWTH TRENDS

(a) Growth is still generally toward metropolitan areas. During the 1960's metropolitan counties continued to grow more rapidly than their nonmetropolitan counterparts.

Population Change 1960-1966

	Per Cent Increase in Population	Average Annual Per Cent Increase in Population
United States	9.3%	1.4%
Nonmetropolitan Counties	6.0	0.9
Metropolitan Counties	10.9	1.7

(b) Metropolitan areas between 200,000 and 2 million are growing well above the national average. Areas less than 200,000 and areas more than 2 million are growing at the national average or below it.

Source: U.S. Bureau of the Census, *Population Estimates and Projections: Estimates of the Population of Counties in Metropolitan Areas, July 1, 1966, a Summary Report,* Series P-25, No. 427, Washington, D.C., July 31, 1969.

(c) The SMSA's of the Northeast represent the largest concentration of population in the United States.

Metropolitan Population as Per Cent of Total Population by Region 1940-1960

Year	U.S.	Northeast	North Central	South	West
1940	55.1	78.8	52.8	34.5	62.0
1950	59.0	79.1	56.5	41.2	67.0
1960	63.0	79.0	60.1	48.1	71.8

Source: U.S. Bureau of the Census, *Population Estimates: Projection of a Population of Metropolitan Areas—1975,* Series P-25, No. 415, Washington, D.C., January 31, 1969.

65.

(d) Metropolitan areas in the West are growing considerably faster than the national metropolitan average of 10.9 per cent. Four of the five fastest growing metropolitan areas are in the West. Las Vegas leads the way with a population increase between 1960 and 1966 of 85.5 per cent.

Per Cent Change in Population 1960-1966

Region	Metropolitan Areas	Nonmetropolitan Areas
Northeast	6.9%	7.2%
North Central	7.9	2.9
South	14.3	7.0
West	17.9	9.1

Source: U.S. Bureau of the Census, *Population Estimates and Projections: Estimates of the Population of Counties in Metropolitan Areas, July 1, 1966, a Summary Report*, Series P-25, No. 427, Washington, D.C., July 31, 1969.

DISPARITIES AMONG SMSA'S

I. POPULATION

The SMSA's range in population from approximately 70,000 (Midland, Texas) to more than 11 million (New York SMSA).

SMSA's—1966

Total Population	No. of SMSA's
2,000,000 and over	11
1,000,000-2,000,000	19
500,000-1,000,000	36
200,000-500,000	76
100,000-200,000	61
under 100,000	18

Source: U.S. Bureau of the Census, *Population Estimates and Projections: Estimates of the Population of Counties in Metropolitan Areas, July 1, 1966, a Summary Report*, Series P-25, No. 427, Washington, D.C., July 31, 1969.

66.

II. INCOME

In 1966 the "average" SMSA had a total personal income of $2 billion and a per capita income of $3,314.

However, total personal income varies from $109 million in Laredo, Texas to $46 billion in the New York SMSA. Per capita income varies from $1,300 in McAllen-Pharr-Edinburg, Texas to more than $4,000 in the Paterson-Passaic-Clifton, New Jersey SMSA.

The seven largest SMSA's (New York, Los Angeles-Long Beach, Chicago, Philadelphia, Detroit, San Francisco-Oakland, Boston) together accounted for close to 25 per cent of all income in the United States in 1966. With approximately 20 per cent of the population, these SMSA's had an average income of about $3,800, nearly 25 per cent more than that of other SMSA's.

In 1966, more than 63 per cent of the SMSA's had a total income of less than $1 billion.

Income Size (1966) (in millions)	No. of SMSA's
Less than $499	73
$ 500-$ 999	68
$ 1,000-$ 1,999	36
$ 2,000-$ 2,999	14
$ 3,000-$ 3,999	10
$ 4,000-$ 4,999	7
$ 5,000-$ 9,999	8
$10,000-$49,999	7

Source: Robert E. Graham, Jr. and Edwin J. Coleman, "Metropolitan Area Incomes, 1929-66," in Survey of Current Business, August 1968.

I. POPULATION

During the past half century the internal shifts in population have been altering the distribution of population within the SMSA's.

Distribution of SMSA Population between
Central Cities and Outside Central Cities 1900-1965

Year	Per Cent of SMSA Population Within the Central City	Per Cent of SMSA Population Outside the Central City
1900	62.2%	37.8%
1910	64.6	35.4
1920	66.0	34.0
1930	64.6	35.4
1940	62.7	37.3
1950	58.7	41.3
1960	51.4	48.6
1965	48.1	51.9

Source: Alan K. Campbell and Seymour Sacks. *Metropolitan America* (New York: The Free Press, 1967).

II. RACE

Proportion of Population in SMSA's that is Nonwhite 1900-1965

Year	Per Cent Nonwhite in the Central City	Per Cent Nonwhite Outside the Central City
1900	6.8%	9.4%
1910	6.9	8.1
1920	7.3	7.0
1930	9.0	6.4
1940	10.1	6.0
1950	13.1	5.7
1960	17.8	5.2
1965	20.8	5.0

Source: Alan K. Campbell and Seymour Sacks. *Metropolitan America* (New York: The Free Press, 1967).

III. CENTRAL CITY AND OUTSIDE CENTRAL CITY INCOMES

Families living outside the central city received greater income than those families living within the central city in 1964.

1964	Central City	Outside Central City
Median Family Income	$6,700	$7,800
Per Cent of Families with Incomes Less than $3,000	15%	10%
Per Cent of Families with Incomes More than $10,000	24%	31%

Source: U.S. Bureau of the Census, *Consumer Income—Income in 1964 of Families and Unrelated Individuals by Metropolitan/Nonmetropolitan Residence,* Series P-60, No. 48, Washington, D.C., April 25, 1966.

The Metropolitan
Toronto Experience

The Municipality of Metropolitan Toronto, with a population of more than 2,000,000, is the focal point of one of North America's most economically vital regions. Metropolitan Toronto contains almost 10 per cent of the total population of Canada, and its 241 square miles contain approximately 11 per cent of all Canadian employment. While, in terms of population, it is not of the magnitude of a New York or Los Angeles, Metropolitan Toronto does approximate the size of a Cleveland, Pittsburgh, or St. Louis. In fact, today it is one of the 20 most populous urban areas in North America.

Metropolitan Toronto has been termed a "boom town" and rightly so. The population of the metropolitan area has grown by about 75 per cent in the last 15 years, and the increases of nearly 55,000 persons per year represent an annual growth rate of over 4 per cent, one of the highest such rates among major metropolitan areas on the continent. Most of this development in the past several years has taken place in three large suburban municipalities—Etobicoke, North York, and Scarborough. In 1953 the City of Toronto had 57 per cent of the total population in the metropolitan area compared with 43 per cent in the suburbs. By 1969 the situation was reversed; the city had only 35 per cent of the total metropolitan population and the suburbs 65 per cent. During this period, Etobicoke's percentage increased from 6 per cent to 14 per cent. Scarborough's from 7 per cent to 15 per cent, and North York's from 9 per cent to 23 per cent.

This remarkable growth has not occurred without its problems and crises. Yet such matters are not unique to this area but rather are indicative of the problems associated with urban growth and expansion now facing *most* urban areas in North America. However, the approach to dealing adequately with these problems *is* unique. Indeed, it represents a major breakthrough in governmental structure. Hopefully, the Toronto experience—modified to suit the needs of individual areas—can serve as a guide to metropolitan governmental reform in the United States.

THE TORONTO REGION: ITS EVOLUTION AND DEVELOPMENT

As the population of the Toronto region grew during the last half of the 19th century, many small towns and villages developed outside the city proper but in close proximity to it. The city met this urban expansion on its borders in a customary fashion—by annexing these suburbs. Beginning in 1883 there was an annexation every few years of one of these suburbs. This procedure of absorbing adjacent areas continued almost unabated until the start of World War I.

In 1928 the Toronto City Council enunciated its unwritten policy which had existed since 1914: that there would be no further annexations of suburban lands. This announcement heralded a new type of political development on the urban fringes; for as areas contiguous to the City of Toronto became urban in character, they did not look forward, as they once did, to annexation by the city. Instead they developed their own municipal structures. By 1930 there were 13 independent and separate municipalities in the Toronto area—the central city (Toronto), five townships (York, North York, East York, Etobicoke, Scarborough), four towns (Leaside, Weston, Mimico, New Toronto), and three villages (Forest Hill, Long Branch, Swansea).

During the period of the 1930's, 1940's, and early 1950's, the 13 municipalities, while in close proximity to one another, went their separate ways with but a few exceptions. However, rapid growth and development, which was occurring particularly in the suburbs, affected all. The whole metropolitan area grew haphazardly with the suburban population growing almost five-fold in 20 years. With no comprehensive regional development plan, each municipality sought to provide development geared to a locally conceived plan.

Indeed, the area exhibited most of the now all-too-familiar urban problems facing North American metropolitan areas today. These include: (a) an inability to plan regionally because of governmental fragmentation; (b) the inadequacy of water and sewage facilities for a burgeoning population; (c) the inability to develop modern coordinated public transportation systems; (d) the inability of individual jurisdictions to finance reasonably major projects and programs; and (e) problems dealing with all aspects of the urban environment from the provision of education to the prevention of pollution.

It was plain that in order for the municipal governments in the Metropolitan Toronto area to function effectively a different form of governmental organization would be required.

METROPOLITAN GOVERNMENT—PHASE I

In 1947 the Province of Ontario's first Minister of Planning and Development (now Minister of Municipal Affairs) established the Toronto and Suburban Planning Board. It was the responsibility of this Board to study the problems of water supply, sewage disposal, transportation, the provision of education on an equitable basis, and the establishment of parklands in the Toronto area. Under the chairmanship of Frederick G. Gardiner, this Board (subsequently renamed the Toronto and York Planning Board) issued a report in 1949 recommending the progressive amalgamation of the 13 municipalities.

Two years earlier, in 1947, the Town of Mimico had applied to the Ontario Municipal Board[1] for the creation of a board to administer throughout the area of the 13 municipalities many of the basic

1/The Ontario Municipal Board (O.M.B.) is a quasi-judicial board appointed by the Prime Minister of Ontario to review virtually all aspects of municipal government in the province.

public services which were inter-municipal in character. This application would have maintained the separate identity of the 13 established municipalities.

While the Mimico application was before the O.M.B., the City of Toronto adopted the recommendation of the Toronto and York Planning Board and applied to the Ontario Municipal Board for an order that the 13 municipalities be progressively amalgamated into one municipality. This application was supported by the Town of Mimico, but it suggested that, should Toronto's application be refused, its own application should be considered. The other 11 municipalities opposed Toronto's application in extensive hearings held before the Ontario Municipal Board under the chairmanship of Lorne R. Cumming.

The Cumming Report

After over two years of taking evidence and deliberating, the O.M.B. handed down its decision on January 20, 1953. The landmark decision, known as the Cumming Report, recommended a federal system of government for the Toronto area. It advocated a federation of the 13 municipalities, each retaining its local autonomy while passing over to the metropolitan government the responsibility for major regional services and other matters of common concern.

Shortly after the release of the Cumming Report, a bill to institute the recommendations of the report was introduced in the Ontario Legislature by the Prime Minister of the Province of Ontario. In this way the provincial government threw its full support behind the proposal for a metropolitan government. Less than three months later, on April 15, 1953, the Ontario Legislature passed "Bill 80" or the Municipality of Metropolitan Toronto Act. The first urban federation in North America came into being on January 1, 1954.

Metropolitan Council

The Metropolitan Council was composed of 24 members (exclusive of the Chairman), 12 from the city and 12 from the suburbs, with all committees being similarly balanced. Members of the Metropolitan Council were not elected directly but rather derived their seats by virtue of holding elective office in their own municipalities. The Council was to elect annually a Chairman who might or might not be an elected representative of a municipality. However, the province appointed the first Chairman, Frederick G. Gardiner.

Shared Powers and Responsibilities

The Metropolitan Corporation—established by the 1953 legislation—and its various departments, boards, and commissions were set up to provide those basic services which transcended the boundaries of the individual municipalities. The area municipalities, however, retained the responsibility for local services and facilities. The extent and quality of these services, within limits, were left to the discretion of the local councils.

Powers over certain functions were retained exclusively by the metropolitan government. These included assessment of property, construction and maintenance of expressways, and the development of regional parks. Other powers pertaining primarily to local matters, such as street lighting and community centers, were reserved entirely to the municipalities. The form of departmental organization, size of staff, and amount of expenditure per capita varied widely from one municipality to another, reflecting the basic autonomy of local government operations within the metropolitan framework. But for almost every metropolitan service, such as roads, water supply, sewage disposal, parks, and traffic control, the powers were shared, with the metropolitan government concentrating on the area-wide needs and the individual municipalities on their own requirements. This interrelationship is best illustrated by examining the division of powers between the local municipalities and the metropolitan government with respect to specific functions.

Finance. The operation of the metropolitan government is based on the pooling of the financial resources of the area municipalities through a system of metropolitan assessment and taxation. The Metropolitan Corporation annually levies its requirements for funds on the basis of each municipality's share of the total assessment of the metropolitan area. However, the Metropolitan Corporation has no power to collect taxes directly and thus the metropolitan levy and those

74.

of the metropolitan and local school boards are included in the local tax bill collected by each municipality. Conversely, the local municipalities do not have the power to borrow money directly. As a result, their requirements for debenture financing are submitted to the Metropolitan Council, which determines the total amount of money to be borrowed for local purposes each year and the proportion to be allocated to each municipality. Thus, all debentures are issued by the Metropolitan Corporation which borrows money on its own account and in behalf of the area municipalities. This means that the local municipalities by themselves no longer face the risks of the money market or shoulder the burden of major inter-municipal projects.

Water Supply. The construction and maintenance of pumping stations, filtration plants, trunk mains, and reservoirs for the wholesale distribution of water to the municipalities is a metropolitan responsibility. The Metropolitan Corporation sells water to the local municipalities on a wholesale basis, while the local distribution systems and the retail of water to consumers remain the responsibility of the local municipalities.

Transportation. The Metropolitan Corporation assumed jurisdiction over all major roads and established an arterial system of highways. The local municipalities continued to maintain minor collectors and local roads in their respective areas. With assumption of the arterial system, the metropolitan government has been able to institute an area-wide traffic control system which is one of the most advanced in North America and which has yielded significant results in terms of greater safety and more efficient traffic flows. All public transit (except trains, planes, and taxis) in the metropolitan area is operated by the Toronto Transit Commission, whose members are appointed by the Metropolitan Council. The public transit system comprises an integrated network of subway, street car, and bus lines which carries over one million passengers on an average weekday.

Planning. The control of development of the area in and adjacent to Metropolitan Toronto was deemed of such importance that the province in the Metropolitan Toronto Act established the Metropolitan Toronto Planning Area, containing 720 square miles and comprising the 13 municipalities in Metropolitan Toronto and 13 surrounding municipalities. In this way it was felt that the Metropolitan Planning Board could guide development on a rational regional scale. The Planning Board was to study matters relating to the development of the area, to prepare an official plan, to advise the Metropolitan Council and other area councils, and to provide public information. Under the legislation, the preparation of official plans and subdivision control were shared responsibilities; zoning (except adjacent to metropolitan roads), redevelopment, land division, and building bylaws were reserved to the local municipalities. The Metropolitan Planning Board also has been concerned with the maintenance of basic planning standards and principles considered to be of area-wide significance.

Additional Responsibilities

Since its formation the metropolitan government has extended its jurisdiction into fields not covered in the original 1953 legislation.

Police. In 1957 the 13 area police forces were amalgamated into one metropolitan force. Earlier, the individual municipalities operated their own police forces, which varied greatly in terms of the number of officers, the area served, and the ratio of officers to residents. In addition, there was no central communications system to facilitate coordination among different police forces.

Today the Metropolitan Police Department is organized into five districts which cover the metropolitan area with no regard for local boundaries. This has eliminated artificial service areas and has aided in the integration of communications systems and the standardization of regulations and procedures.

Licensing. The Metropolitan Licensing Commission was created in 1957 to establish area-wide standards and regulations for a variety of trades and services that had previously been licensed separately by the individual area municipalities. Earlier, licensing regulations had varied widely within the area, and not all the local municipalities had licensing boards. Fees also had varied widely across the metropolitan area. Today the Commission controls the licensing of some 90 different activities.

76.

METROPOLITAN GOVERNMENT—PHASE II

During the first ten years of its existence the metropolitan government was the subject of both praise and criticism. One point of contention rested on the fact that although the 12 suburban municipalities varied greatly in terms of population—Weston had some 10,000 persons while North York had 360,000—they each had only one representative on the Metropolitan Council. The need for a complete appraisal of the metropolitan system appeared in order. Thus, in April 1963, Prime Minister Robarts of Ontario announced the appointment of a one-man Royal Commission, under the chairmanship of H. Carl Goldenberg, to provide an independent assessment and evaluation of all aspects of the metropolitan federation.

The Goldenberg Report

In June 1965 the Royal Commissioner issued the findings of his two-year inquiry. He had two basic recommendations: (1) that the metropolitan system of government be retained, and (2) that the 13 municipalities be consolidated into four cities. The Goldenberg Report and its recommendations were the subject of considerable discussion and debate. This is reflected in the statement of Prime Minister Robarts on the introduction of the Metropolitan Toronto Amendment Act of 1966:

> *While the position of the Government may not coincide with the recommendations of Dr. Goldenberg on all points, we accept and endorse the main principles which he advocates: the continuation of the two-level federated system of Metropolitan Government; the consolidation of constituent municipalities rather than total amalgamation; an increase in the authority and responsibilities of the Government of Metropolitan Toronto; a Metro-wide uniform tax levy to provide a basic education program for the Metropolitan area; and a reform of the system of representation.*[1]

Although the provincial government accepted certain recommendations of the Goldenberg Report, it modified some and rejected others. Again, the provincial government exercised its prerogative.

1/*The Telegram,* Toronto, January 10, 1966, p. 9.

The New Metropolitan Government

The final outcome was the Metropolitan Toronto Amendment Act of 1966 (Bill 81) which created, effective January 1, 1967, a new metropolitan government by consolidating the 13 municipalities into five boroughs and one city: the *Borough of East York*—East York, Leaside; the *Borough of North York*—North York; the *Borough of Etobicoke*—Etobicoke, New Toronto, Long Branch, Mimico; the *Borough of Scarborough*—Scarborough; the *Borough of York*—York, Weston; and the *City of Toronto*—Toronto, Forest Hill, Swansea.

Metropolitan Council

In addition, the composition of the Metropolitan Council was altered to provide for a 33-member body, including the Chairman, elected on a representative population basis. East York now has 2 members on the Council; York, 3; Etobicoke, 4; Scarborough, 5; North York, 6; and Toronto, 12. What was once a city-suburban split of 12-12 was altered to a 20-12 division in favor of the suburbs. The policy-recommending body of the Council, its Executive Committee, now consists of the Metropolitan Chairman, the six local municipal mayors, and the two senior controllers and two aldermen from the City of Toronto Council. Thus, in the Executive Committee the even (5-5) division remains. In case of a deadlock the Metropolitan Chairman has the deciding vote. The term of office for these elected officials was also extended from two to three years.

Responsibilities

The new metropolitan government was given several new responsibilities, and some of the functions for which it was already responsible were broadened by the new provincial legislation. Each of the new or expanded functions noted below exemplifies the sharing of power between the local municipalities and the metropolitan government.

Education. Despite an impressive record in providing school accommodation, there were continuing wide disparities in the burden of school costs. Therefore, the basic function of the Metropolitan School Board was altered from providing local boards of education with maintenance payments to providing them, through a metropolitan-wide levy, with funds necessary for a basic metropolitan-wide education program.

Under the new system, the Metropolitan School Board which previously had been equally divided between the city and suburban members, now comprises six representatives from the City School Board, nine from the suburban boards and three from the Separate School Board. Each of the six local municipalities has retained its own elected board of education which is responsible for administering the local public school system. The Metropolitan School Board is responsible for receiving, altering, approving, or rejecting the operating budgets of the local boards of education; for receiving and distributing all provincial grants for school purposes; and for otherwise raising the money to finance the local school systems through taxation. A local board of education may levy a supplementary school tax on its own municipality to a maximum of 1.5 mills for public school purposes and 1 mill for secondary school purposes.

While the local boards retain autonomy in operating their individual school systems, the Metropolitan School Board exercises certain important functions in addition to its basic responsibility in financial matters. For example, it has the power to set attendance areas, and in this way problems created by artificial municipal boundaries can be overcome. Moreover, the Metropolitan Board pays the full cost of classes for handicapped children and operates the Metropolitan School for the Deaf.

Welfare. Since a large proportion of the total metropolitan welfare load originated in the City of Toronto, a severe financial burden had been placed on the city. As a result, beginning in 1964 the Metropolitan Corporation voluntarily undertook to pay the local share (20 per cent local, 80 per cent provincial) of welfare assistance payments while the administration of the programs remained in local hands. This arrangement ensured that the burden of meeting the cost of mandatory welfare programs under provincial legislation would be spread across the metropolitan area, but it left the local municipalities responsible for a variety of optional services. In 1967 public welfare became solely the responsibility of the metropolitan government. This arrangement made it possible officially to provide a more uniform level of service in all parts of the area and helped to ensure that the needs of the inhabitants could be met regardless of their place of residence.

Refuse Collection and Disposal. In 1967 the responsibility for disposal of refuse and industrial wastes was assumed by the Metropolitan Corporation, while leaving collection as a local responsibility.

ACCOMPLISHMENTS
OF THE METROPOLITAN SYSTEM

Metropolitan government has achieved many things in its comparatively short period of operation. Specifically, it has solved the water and sewage problems by the construction of new sewage treatment plants, pumping stations, water filtration plants, and by the installation of many miles of large trunk sewers and trunk watermains. Transportation has also been vastly improved; today there is an integrated system of public and private, rapid and conventional modes of transport. There is now a centralized police force, and a 5,000 acre regional park system is under development. In addition, a metropolitan plan has been adopted to guide regional expansion on a rational basis.

The pooling of financial resources at the metropolitan level has provided a base from which projects, facilities, and programs beneficial to the entire area have been developed. Without this, it would have been impossible to provide for the expansion in services required by the region's growth. Not only has the metropolitan system supplied vast flows of capital funds, but it also has maintained the highest possible rating on Wall Street for foreign municipal bonds. It has been estimated that the resultant lower interest rates meant a saving between 1954 and 1967 of approximately $50 million.[1]

Finally, without doubt the most important factor in Toronto's success has been the guidance and stimulus provided by the provincial government. Without this catalytic agent it is highly unlikely that the Toronto area would have metropolitan government today.

---

[1]/James Nathan Miller, "Metro: Toronto's Answer to Urban Sprawl," *The Reader's Digest*, August 1967.

Municipality of Metropolitan Toronto   ...comprising Six Municipalities

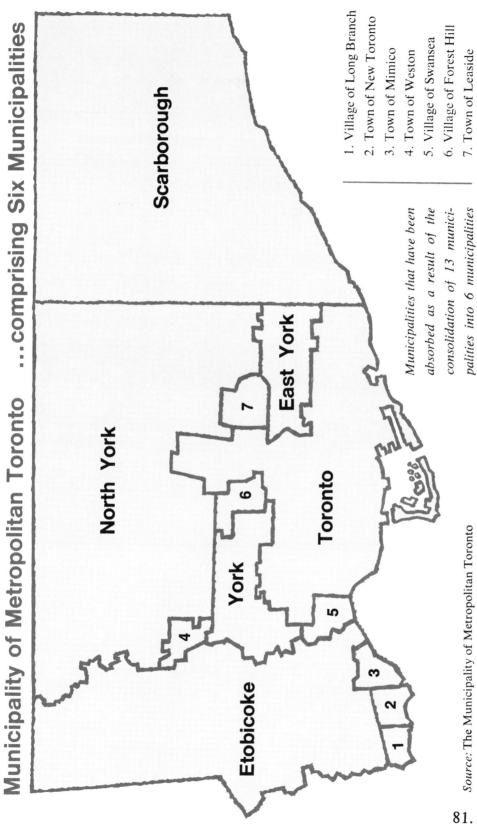

1. Village of Long Branch
2. Town of New Toronto
3. Town of Mimico
4. Town of Weston
5. Village of Swansea
6. Village of Forest Hill
7. Town of Leaside

Municipalities that have been absorbed as a result of the consolidation of 13 munici-palities into 6 municipalities

Source: The Municipality of Metropolitan Toronto

Municipality of Metropolitan Toronto comprising Six Municipalities

Municipality	Square Miles	Population		Members on Council
		Persons	Per Cent	
City of Toronto (City, Swansea, Forest Hill)	37.7	720,000	37	12
Borough of North York (North York)	68.1	475,000	21	6
Borough of Scarborough (Scarborough)	70.0	310,000	15	5
Borough of Etobicoke (Etobicoke, Long Branch, New Toronto, Mimico)	47.9	290,000	14	4
Borough of York (York, Weston)	9.0	150,000	8	3
Borough of East York (East York, Leaside)	8.3	105,000	5	2
Metropolitan Toronto	241.0	2,050,000	100	32

82.

Distribution of Responsibility
M—*Municipality of Metropolitan Toronto*
A—*Area Municipalities*

Finance and Taxation		Water Supply		Health	
Assessment of property	M	*Purification, pumping and trunk distribution system*	M	*Public health services*	A
Courts of revision	MA			*Chronic and convalescent hospital*	M
Taxation of property	A	*Local distribution*	A	*Hospital grants*	A
Debenture borrowing	M	*Collection of water bills*	A	*Ambulance services*	M
Local improvement charges	A	**Sewage Disposal**		**Police and Fire Protection**	
Planning		*Sanitary trunk system and disposal plants*	M	*Police*	M
Official plans	MA	*Connecting systems*	A	*Fire*	A
Subdivision approval	MA	*Storm drainage*	MA	**Administration of Justice**	
Zoning	A	**Garbage Collection and Disposal**			
Recreation/ Community Services				*Magistrates' courts*	M
		Collection	A	*Court house and jail*	M
Regional parks	M	*Disposal sites*	M	*Juvenile and family court*	M
Local parks	A	**Air Pollution**		*Coroner's office*	M
Recreation programs	A			*Registry and land titles offices*	M
Community centres/ arenas	A	*Air pollution control*	M		
Municipal golf courses	M	**Public Education**		**Licensing and Inspection**	
Municipal zoo	M				
Regional libraries	M	*Operation of school system*	A	*Business licensing*	M
Local libraries	MA	*School sites, attendance areas, building programs*	M	*Dog licensing and pound*	A
Grants to cultural societies	MA			*Marriage licenses*	A
Road Construction/ Maintenance		*Operating and capital costs*	M	*Buildings by-laws*	A
Expressways	M	**Housing**		**Civil Defense**	
Arterial roads	M				
Local roads	A	*Low rental family housing*	M	*Emergency measures*	M
Bridges and grade separations	MA	*Elderly person housing*	M	**Other Municipal Services**	
Snow removal	MA	*Moderate rental family housing*	A		
Street cleaning	MA			*Collection of fines*	MA
Sidewalks	A	**Welfare**		*Collection of vital statistics*	A
Traffic Control				*Distribution of hydro power*	A
Traffic regulations	MA	*Welfare assistance*	M	*Harbor*	A
Cross-walks	MA	*Hospitalization of indigents*	M	*Island airport*	A
Traffic lights	M			*Municipal parking lots*	A
Street lighting	A	*Assistance to Children's Aid Societies*	M	*Preparation of voters' lists and administration of civic elections*	A
Pavement markings	MA				
Public Transit		*Homes for the aged*	M	*Redevelopment*	MA
Toronto Transit Comm.	M				

37349

83.

PUBLICATION ORDER FORM

To order CED publications please indicate number in column entitled "# Copies Desired." Then mail this order form and check for total amount in envelope to Distribution Division, CED, 477 Madison Ave., New York 10022.

ORDER NUMBER	STATEMENTS ON NATIONAL POLICY *(paper bound)*		# COPIES DESIRED

35P . . RESHAPING GOVERNMENT IN METROPOLITAN AREAS $1.00 _____
Recommends a two-level system of government for metropolitan areas: an area-wide level and a community level comprised of "community districts." Provides a brief description of problems in metropolitan areas which severely limit the quality of life and demonstrates ways in which the existing governmental structure stands in the way of their solution.

34P . . ASSISTING DEVELOPMENT IN LOW-INCOME COUNTRIES $1.25 _____
Offers a sound rationale for public support of the U.S. economic assistance program and recommends a far-ranging set of priorities for U.S. Government policy. The statement proposes better ways by which the U.S. and other advanced nations can speed the growth of low-income countries through the application of public and private external resources—financial, managerial, and technological.

33P . . NONTARIFF DISTORTIONS OF TRADE $1.00 _____
Examines the complex problem of dealing with nontariff distortions of trade arising from governmental measures that create special barriers to imports and incentives to exports. Recommends that GATT serve as the forum for negotiating the reduction of these obstacles to the free flow of trade as it has in the case of tariffs. Statement was developed jointly with CED counterpart organizations in Europe, Japan, and Australia.

32P . . FISCAL AND MONETARY POLICIES FOR STEADY ECONOMIC GROWTH $1.00 _____
Reexamines the role of fiscal and monetary policies in achieving the basic economic objectives of high employment, price stability, economic growth, and equilibrium in the nation's international payments. Deals with the argument that to achieve high employment the economy must tolerate some degree of unemployment. Urges that early each year the Congress review the total impact of the federal budget to determine if specific fiscal action, affecting expenditures and tax rates, must be taken for stabilization purposes.

31 P . . FINANCING A BETTER ELECTION SYSTEM $1.00 _____
Urges comprehensive modernization of election and campaign procedures at national, state, and local levels. Proposes ways to reduce costs and spread them more widely through tax credits. Calls for full public disclosure of all aspects of political finance to inhibit excesses and abuses.

30 P . . INNOVATION IN EDUCATION $1.00 _____
Concludes that four measures are imperative if the shortcomings of today's elementary and secondary education are to be overcome: 1) better organization of the schools for innovation and change; 2) increased emphasis on both basic and applied educational research and on the dissemination of research; 3) utilization by school systems of cost-benefit and cost-effectiveness analysis; and 4) creation of a national commission on educational research and innovation.

29 P . . THE NATIONAL ECONOMY AND THE VIETNAM WAR $1.00 _____
Offers a broad program to deal with growing inflation, the increasing balance-of-payments deficit, and the continued attack on the dollar. Shows how the nation has faltered in dealing with the economic impact of the rapid increase in government spending for Vietnam. Discusses the economic transition from war to peace.

28P . . MODERNIZING STATE GOVERNMENT $1.00 _____
Recommends sweeping renovation of state governments and their constitutions. Proposes granting legislatures broad powers to deal with problems of a rapidly-changing era; strengthening executive capability through modern management methods; improving the administration of justice; and furthering beneficial intergovernmental relations.

27 P . . TRADE POLICY TOWARD LOW-INCOME COUNTRIES $1.50 _____
Presents 12 recommendations concerning trade policies of the high-income countries toward the low-income countries. It includes specific proposals to help increase the export earnings of the world's developing regions. Statement was developed jointly with CED counterpart organizations in Europe and Japan.

26 P . . A FISCAL PROGRAM FOR A BALANCED FEDERALISM $1.00 _____
This statement considers what should be done by state and local governments to increase their fiscal authority and responsibility so they can meet the rapidly growing demand for public services. It also suggests how a partial federal income tax credit for individuals who pay state income taxes could be used to increase the fiscal capacity of the states.

25 P . . THE DOLLAR AND THE WORLD MONETARY SYSTEM $1.50 _____
Analyzes the U.S. balance-of-payments problem in relation to our national and international goals. Explains the key role of the dollar in the international monetary system. Recommends measures, including restraint of domestic demand, to reduce U.S. balance-of-payments deficits. Discusses the various proposals for international monetary reform.

24 P . . HOW LOW INCOME COUNTRIES CAN ADVANCE THEIR OWN GROWTH $1.50 _____
Describes the internal aspects of economic development and the essential requirements for achieving sustained high rates of growth in per capita income, drawn from the experience of the low income countries. Includes a statement on Latin America by the Inter-American Council for Commerce and Production. (also in Spanish)

23 P . . MODERNIZING LOCAL GOVERNMENT $1.00 _____
A hard-hitting analysis of the need for better local government so that towns, counties, cities, and suburbs can cope with present day conditions — with a series of recommendations for structural changes that would alleviate the severe and increasing social, political, and financial strains on these governments.

SEE OTHER SIDE >

22 P . . A BETTER BALANCE IN FEDERAL TAXES ON BUSINESS 75¢ _____

This statement urges consideration of a federal value-added tax on business to meet increasing defense expenditures and to avert inflation. It proposes a value-added tax as a permanent part of the tax structure, and that this tax should substitute for a part of the corporate income tax as soon as revenue conditions permit.

21 P . . BUDGETING FOR NATIONAL OBJECTIVES $1.00 _____

The federal budgeting process should be used as the essential instrument for defining and achieving national purposes. Both executive and legislative branches can employ the budget more effectively to reach rational policy and program decisions and to ensure efficient management.

19 P . . EAST-WEST TRADE: A COMMON POLICY FOR THE WEST $1.00 _____

An examination and analysis of the special problems to be faced in considering expanded trade relations with the communist countries. Study was developed jointly with CED counterpart organizations in France, Germany, Italy, and Japan.

18 P . . DEVELOPING METROPOLITAN TRANSPORTATION POLICIES $1.00 _____

This statement is a guide for local leaders to help them understand transportation problems, the choices available, and how to obtain information.

16 P . . ECONOMIC DEVELOPMENT OF CENTRAL AMERICA $1.25 _____

Surveys the impact of the Central American Common Market and outlines new steps to be taken to speed economic growth in the area. Includes a summary of agrarian reform laws. Spanish and English text on facing pages.

15 P . . EDUCATING TOMORROW'S MANAGERS $1.00 _____

Seeks to increase public understanding of the functions of business schools and departments in American colleges and universities. Indicates ways in which educators and businessmen can combine their efforts to serve the interests of students, business, institutions of learning, and our society as a whole.

14 P . . IMPROVING EXECUTIVE MANAGEMENT IN THE FEDERAL GOVERNMENT $1.50 _____

Calls for major reforms in the selection, development, compensation, and utilization of the 8600 career executives and professionals who direct the work of the more than 5 million civilian and military personnel in the federal government.

11 P . . JAPAN IN THE FREE WORLD ECONOMY $1.50 _____

Review of Japan's economic growth and its trade relations with 7 recommendations for strengthening economic ties among Japan, the U.S. and other free nations. Japanese views on the same issues are dealt with in a special supplement by Keizai Doyukai (the Japanese CED).

10 P . . AN ADAPTIVE PROGRAM FOR AGRICULTURE $1.00 _____

A five-year program based on the withdrawal of inefficiently used resources (especially labor) from agriculture pointing the way to a saving for taxpayers of $3 billion annually.

9 P . . ECONOMIC LITERACY FOR AMERICANS 75¢ _____

An objective appraisal of the present state of economic literacy in the United States and a realistic plan for improving it.

1 P . . ECONOMIC GROWTH IN THE UNITED STATES $1.00 _____

A Statement on National Policy by the Research and Policy Committee first issued in 1958; updated and reissued by the Program Committee, October 1969.

10-24 copies — 10% discount
25-49 copies — 15% discount

50-99 copies — 20% discount
100-249 copies — 30% discount

☐ *Please bill me (Please remit for orders under $3.00)* TOTAL _____

NOTE TO EDUCATORS: Instructors in colleges and universities may obtain for teaching purposes up to 5 copies of each *Statement on National Policy* free of charge. In excess of 5 copies, the regular educational discount of 20% will apply.

DO YOU WANT ALL CED PUBLICATIONS AS SOON AS ISSUED?

☐ Please send me full particulars on annual CED Forum *membership plan*.

☐ Please send me newest list of all CED publications.

☐ Please send me newest list of CED *international library* items published by CED counterpart organizations in Europe, Japan, Latin America, and Australia.

☐ Businessman ☐ Educator ☐ Professional

Name...

Address...

City...State...Zip..